The Passion-Driven Classroom

A Framework for Teaching & Learning

Angela Maiers
Amy Sandvold

EYE ON EDUCATION
6 DEPOT WAYWEST, SUITE 106
LARCHMONT, NY 10538
(914) 833–0551
(914) 833–0761 fax
www.eyeoneducation.com

A sincere effort has been made to supply the identity of those who have created specific strategies. Any omissions have been unintentional.

Library of Congress Cataloging-in-Publication Data

Maiers, Angela.
  The passion-driven classroom : a framework for teaching & learning /
Angela Maiers, Amy Sandvold.
      p. cm.
  ISBN 978-1-59667-159-1
 1. Motivation in education. 2. Classroom environment. 3. Effective
teaching. 4. Teachers--In-service training. I. Sandvold, Amy, 1971- II.
Title.
  LB1065.M277 2010
  370.15′4--dc22

                                                            2010031658

10 9 8 7 6 5 4 3 2 1

Production services provided by
Rick Soldin a Book/Print Production Specialist
www.book-comp.com

Also Available from Eye On Education

Battling Boredom:
99 Strategies to Spark Student Engagement
Bryan Harris

What Great Teachers Do *Differently*:
14 Things That Matter Most
Todd Whitaker

Seven Simple Secrets:
What the BEST Teachers Know and Do!
Annette Breaux and Todd Whitaker

Great Quotes for Great Educators
Todd Whitaker and Dale Lumpa

Classroom Motivation from A to Z
Barbara R. Blackburn

101 Poems for Teachers
Annette L. Breaux

101 "Answers" for New Teachers and Their Mentors:
Effective Teaching Tips for Daily Classroom Use
Annette L. Breaux

50 Ways to Improve Student Behavior:
Simple Solutions to Complex Challenges
Annette Breaux and Todd Whitaker

**How the Best Teachers Avoid the
20 Most Common Teaching Mistakes**
Elizabeth Breaux

How the Best Teachers Differentiate Instruction
Elizabeth Breaux and Monique B. Magee

Teaching, Learning, and Assessment Together:
Reflective Assessments
Arthur K. Ellis et al.

**What Do You Say When…?
Best Practice Language for Improving Student Behavior**
Hal Holloman and Peggy H. Yates

We give special thanks to our families. When you agree to write a book your whole family agrees to write the book! Thank you for hanging in there through countless working weekends and lonely evenings. Your words of encouragement, unwavering support, and unconditional love kept us going. Our lives are richer because of all of you.

From Angela: Bob, you are my rock. For twenty years you have allowed me to chase my dreams, no matter how crazy. You are my best friend and my inspiration.

Ryan and Abby, being your mom is the greatest honor in the world. You have filled my life with immense joy and pride. This book represents the classroom that I wish for you.

From Amy: Thanks to Jeff for letting me do my thing again, and to Houston, Andrew, Anna and Lauren for inspiring me to change how I teach. This book exists because of you. This book is also dedicated to Sr. Norma Jean Holthaus, a true model of a passion-driven leader and colleague.

Contents

About the Authors

Angela Maiers a is a 20-year career educator. She is currently working as an independent consultant dedicated and committed to helping State Departments of Education, schools, districts and teachers to reach their goals in literacy and literacy education.

She is fortunate for the opportunities and extensive experiences she has had working with educators. Angela spends her time teaching, researching, writing, speaking, and conducting seminars across the country in the areas of literacy, learning, and 21st century education. Her work is featured in the *National Research Council Yearbook,* multiple professional journals, and most recently in *Urban Schools Most Promising Practices,* published by the International Reading Association.

She is also an author of several books, articles, and curriculum support materials and continually strives to connect research and scientific theory to real world practices. Her classroom demonstrations and direct work with students keeps Angela grounded in ensuring that the research base stays within the context of real classrooms and schools.

For the past decade, she has created and organized multiple literacy institutes reaching thousands of educators across the United States. These summer institutes provide an innovative and unique venue for educators, administrators, and curriculum developers. Every student reaches their highest literacy and learning potential when they are led by such knowledgeable and passionate leaders.

Connecting higher education and the work done in schools, she has spent years working at the undergraduate and graduate level teaching courses in reading, content area reading, emergent literacy, and assessment.

She received her bachelor's degree from The University of Iowa and did both her graduate and post graduate work at Drake University.

Angela currently lives in Clive, Iowa with her husband and two children, Ryan and Abigail and the family dog, Buttons.

www.angelamaiers.com

Amy Sandvold is an administrator, teacher and learner. She has served in both public and parochial schools in rural, urban and suburban areas. She has worked in Title I Reading, 3rd and 5th grades, and served as a full-time literacy coach of teachers. She has been an Education Programs/School Improvement Consultant for the Iowa Department of Education and has taught several courses at the University of Northern Iowa.

Currently, Amy is an Elementary/Middle School Principal at Sacred Heart School in the Cedar Valley Catholic School System. She has presented on numerous literacy and school improvement topics at regional and international conferences. Amy is a graduate of the University of Northern Iowa, earning a BA and Master of Arts In Education K-12 Reading Specialist, and has an Advanced Studies Certificate in PreK-12 Educational Leadership. Amy has written for *The Thinking Classroom*, a publication of the International Reading Association and has co-authored a book on literacy coaching, *The Fundamentals of Literacy Coaching* (2008), published by the Association for Supervision of Curriculum Development (ASCD). Her educational interests include innovative & engaging learning frameworks, mobile devices in the classroom, leadership and literacy coaching.

amysandvold@hotmail.com
SandvoldAmyM@twitter.com

Acknowledgements

When you become passionate about something and follow it, you become happy. We are happy today, not just for the completion of this book, but also for the learning that has taken place along the way the conversations that are just beginning. There is not enough space or time to thank all who inspired and supported our journey to make this book a reality. We are grateful to each and every teacher's classroom we visited and worked with, and the many leaders who shared their thinking with us.

You have made it easy to stay passionate about this work, as we have seen your classrooms transformed and teachers reinvigorated about the profession.

Without the commitment of Bob Sickles, our editor, this passion-driven conversation would never have made it into your hands. Bob pushed us with grace and inspired us with his compassion and leadership. Thank you also to Dan Sickles and the entire Eye On Education team for believing in the importance of our book and its methods. We are deeply grateful for your skill and collegiality.

Preface

"Our lives are marked with a series of events, encounters, and turning points that in one way or another stamp our outlook and move us in a direction that shapes us into who we are today."

—Regie Routman

As the co-authors of this book, we lead busy lives and keeping up requires us to wear many hats. We are teachers. We are researchers. We are writers. We are leaders. We are learners. We are moms. We are friends.

Our Journey

The event that inspired this book occurred after we had completed a week of intense training with teachers. We listened, learned, and participated in conversations with them about what they do and what we do, what they would like to do, and what we would like to do. We told stories of what is working in education and shared frustrations about what is not. We spent the week searching for answers to questions that plague our productivity and keep us up at night:

♦ Are we making a difference in our students' lives?

♦ Are we doing all we can to help every student excel?

♦ Is there more to know?

♦ And if so, how will we find the time, manage the tasks, and fit everything in?

♦ Is it even possible?

That afternoon, we set out on a much needed after-the-workshop run. Little did we know that the answers to our most difficult and profound questions (and the makings of the book you hold in your hands) were about to be thrust upon us, like a bolt of lightning shot down from the sky.

As we talked and jogged, we noticed something peculiar. Nearly the entire running path was inundated with the following flyers:

DON'T   kill animals
HER ar   SUM
ANIMALS   we DON'T
WOT YOU   TO   Kill
  Like   PANDS Manted
SNOWleprs   AND
  Leprs   CETUS
        FOXS

Upon closer examination, we discovered this was no ordinary flyer advertising a recent fad. Instead, it was a markers-and-crayon plea to save endangered animals! The teachers inside of us asked, "Who made these? Where did they come from?" People were noticing the mile-long stretch of homemade flyers. Neighbors were stopping, talking, and committing their signatures of support. We knew we had to find the source of this worthy movement. We followed the paper trail directly to Haley, committed researcher and animal rights activist! Haley's parents described for us her 24-hour-a-day passion for these animals. In her mother's words, "She wakes up thinking about animals and dreams about how to save them at night."

We were fortunate enough to be invited into Haley's "learning lab," (which doubles as a bedroom when she decides to sleep) and could immediately see what they were talking about. When Haley is not in pre-school (yes, our young scientist is barely five), she spends her time reading, writing, researching, and planning her next steps. We were honored to be there as she unveiled Phase Two of her plan to bring her concerns for the animals to the world's attention.

When Haley realized that even her tenacious effort to replace the flyers every night was not enough to spread this important message, she designed a T-shirt so her message could accompany her permanently as she became a walking, talking embodiment of her passion.

She explained:

> Only the people who lived near me saw the flyers. I had to reach the people who live across town, and I found a perfect way. My mommy got me these great markers that do not wash off. In case she is too tired to do laundry I made a T-shirt for every day of the week. I wear them everywhere. That way, if we are in the grocery store or at the mall or even walking outside, people will stop and ask me about the animals. It is sooooo great.

Her efforts are working. In her short campaign, she has collected hundreds of signatures and donations. An endangered panda bear cub in China reaps the benefits of her amazing efforts. And to think, she is just getting started!

We came back from our run that day forever changed. Seeing through Haley's eyes has left an indelible mark in our minds and hearts. There is no doubt we are wiser for knowing her, yet our time with Haley was more than inspirational. It stirred in us a reminder to tend and nurture our own passions—calling us to ask difficult questions of ourselves as learners and leaders. Questions like:

♦ How can we stand in front of learners like Haley and tell them to pursue their passions, to write what they know and care about, and use their gifts to change the world...if we are not willing to do the same?

♦ Are we worthy of such a role in our student's and our own children's lives if we have not done everything possible to stand up for what we believe in, defend it publicly, and move forward with causes that matter most?

♦ Do we as leaders and learners have what it takes to pursue our passions all the way? Do we have the ambition, the instinct, self-motivation, and the drive to put passion into practice?

That day, Haley set the bar high. In no uncertain terms, she said, "It's your turn now! "

So, here we are, with Haley's nudging, writing what we are most passionate about and sharing it with the world. We hope our words will stir your heart and soul and remind you of what matters most: changing lives and changing the world. These are the intrinsic reasons that motivated us to choose this work, right?

Like Haley, we intend for this message to stop you in your tracks and convince you to "step off the path" of doing things like they have always been done. We challenge you to join us in the fight to save our world's most endangered cognitive species—passionate learners.

Watch young children at work and play. The learning attributes you see confirm the obvious truth. Nearly every four-year-old has the talents, qualities, and genius-level characteristics of curiosity, adaptability, and passion that Haley emulates. These fearless young learners roam the earth freely for years with no limits or boundaries to learning. They are joyful, excited, and in awesome wonder every day for all that the world has to offer. Then, something happens—they go to school.

Unbridled enthusiasm, engagement, and passion gradually fade. By the time they reach secondary school, these have nearly disappeared. We know good teachers try to make learning fun and engaging. We know that many teachers work hard to make learning mean something, and this makes the trend even more disturbing and our convictions stronger because we know that passionate, caring, and exemplary teachers not only make a difference—they can reverse and prevent this trend.

As teachers, our role is challenging. We operate in a standards-based, data-driven educational era (Hargreaves, 1994). In subtle and in not-so-subtle ways, we are asked to ignore the creative, critical, and powerful force of passion in teaching and learning. Fidelity to the curriculum and preparation for the test have become the priority. We are being asked to remove love and emotion from our instruction. We slowly and wearily set aside our own love for learning and our students as well as passion for the profession. Our teaching has become a prescription as everything is decided for us—from what to teach, when to teach it, and how to assess it. We teach by chapter and unit. Students are tested on their performance and mastery of the content. We have teacher-proofed the curriculum and everything else that goes with it. Tragically, as a result, we have passion-proofed the learning.

We say, NO MORE! It is time to reassert and reinsert the "heart" back into teaching and learning. Our goal in *The Passion-Driven Classroom* is to help you to do just that and to convince you that passion-driven learning will move our students farther and deeper into mastery of content and knowledge than ever imaginable. Our classrooms will move away from prescription-driven to passion-driven learning. Educational scholarship can be achieved only when we allow our hearts and heads to work in tandem rather than as opposing forces.

We have taught far too long without including passion, and that stops here. It is time to demonstrate that we can and will change our education system. Join us. We need you to fight for passion, we need your voices, we need your gifts, and we need YOU in the passion conversation! (The T-shirts are on the way!)

Let the Journey Begin: Saying Yes! to Passion

By now, we hope you are saying, "YES. Sign me up for this passion stuff! This is why I came to this work, this is why I teach, hear me roar! But wait— what about that 'covering' stuff, the curriculum sitting on my shelf, the test dates looming over my shoulder—what about that stuff?"

We recognize those voices, too. We wrote this book to help you answer questions that we know weigh heavily on your heart:

♦ I have to cover standards, or I will lose my job. Where does this passion stuff fit in?

♦ I have so many diverse needs, how do I have time to discover the passions of each individual in my room? What do I do with it once I discover it?

♦ The test, the test, the test. What if we don't meet Annual Yearly Progress?

♦ There is just no way. It all sounds nice, but where do we find the time?

In the chapters ahead, we answer these important questions. We will guide you in creating the conditions through a framework we call "The Clubhouse Classroom" where passion thrives and survives. Creating and sustaining a Passion-Driven Classroom requires us to let go of many of the mindsets and learning paradigms that have dictated our behaviors and actions for nearly a century. It requires us to funnel our energies in the classroom in different ways. You will see how passion is engrained as a way of life.

In Chapter 1, we begin the conversation by addressing the gap that puts our students and our profession most at risk: The Passion Gap. We challenge you, whether you are a teacher, an administrator, a curriculum director, a professor, or a concerned parent, to rethink what we deem as important in the curriculum and refocus how we teach it.

In Chapter 2, we get comfortable with the word "passion." We want you to feel confident and ready to talk about passion and its role in learning and in the world. We clearly define and share our perspectives on passion while untangling the misconceptions and erroneous images often associated with the idea.

In Chapter 3, we introduce you to the Clubhouse Classroom, which mirrors how we discover and practice our passions in the real world through our favorite clubs. We explore the critical attributes that make club learning such a draw and show you how we can harness this powerful learning framework to the classroom.

In Chapters 4, 5, and 6, we lay out the essential elements, behaviors, and expectations needed to transform a learner's energy and passion into scholarly engagement—and invite you to see it in action in student Learning Clubs. We outline the phases needed in order to provide the groundwork and context for the independent and interdependent work that will transpire from day one. Executing the three phases ensures that passion-driven learning will carry throughout the rest of the year. In these chapters, you will see, feel, and experience passion in practice. We walk you step-by-step through the work of developing student mathematicians, scientists, historians, readers, writers, and world communicators. Each section will describe in detail the schedule and the structure for learner roles, assignments, and resources for Clubhouse Learning.

In Chapter 7, we recognize that even with the best-laid plans, a number of challenges face teachers who consider crossing the bridge between traditional practices and passion-driven instruction. This chapter gives you a glimpse of what the passion conversation sounds like for those in the trenches. We let their voices guide us, prepare us, and inspire us for the dialogue we will ignite in our own schools and classrooms.

In Chapter 8, we return to our original premise and commitment to passion-driven learning. We take our conversations with students and share them with you in a way that reminds us of what they really need and what matters most.

We showcase examples of resources and websites on page 45, which will help you match your students to "good-fit technology" and supplement instructions in the Learning Clubs.

Creating passionate, lifelong learners is the most critical objective of education—not a mantra for our letterhead or phrase in our mission statements. It is our work. It is our promise and it is the job we set out to do. So let the journey begin!

1

Achievement Gap Or Passion Gap?

While reformers and policymakers focus on achievement gaps, testing, and accountability, millions of students mentally and emotionally disengage from learning and many gifted teachers leave the field. Ironically, today's schooling is damaging the single most essential component to education—the joy of learning.

Kristen Olson (*Wounded by School*, 2009)

What we claim to want and what we actually reward in practice are two very different things. Our students get mixed signals. Although passion is rarely figured into the achievement equation, students who lack passion, who feel disengaged from the school experience, are at greater risk for dropping out, have low interest, and score low on standardized achievement tests (Osterman, 2000). While we vigorously support high standards, rigorous curriculum, and emphasize critical thinking, problem solving, and intellectual scholarship for our students, we gain little if we have not stirred their hearts.

Listening To Our Students

We know we often fail at reaching the heart, as evidenced in the following list of phrases heard daily from the mouths of our students:

♦ Do we have to do this?

♦ Is this for a grade?

♦ How many pages?

♦ Not again.

- When are we ever going to use this stuff?

- I HATE school! School is jail.

We rarely hear the phrases:

- THIS ROCKS

- Soooo Cool!

- LOVE it!

- Give me more!

- UN-BEEEEE-LIEV-ABLE!!!

- I'm not done yet! I need more time to make it better!

- Wow, you have got to see this!

- This is so amazing—let me show you!

- Look what I learned!

- You will not believe what I can do!

This is cause for alarm. These common and seemingly innocent comments are strong indicators that disengagement from rigorous intellectual endeavor is the norm. They confirm that students are going through the motions, following the rules, and interacting with content that holds little meaning for them. Most compelling is that these simple comments illustrate the canyon-sized gap that exists between the learning we have and the learning we desire. This gap is significantly separated by one intangible, unquantifiable, and undeniably important variable: PASSION.

Merriam and Webster define passion in this way: "intense, driving, or overmastering feeling or conviction," and "a strong liking or desire for or devotion to some activity, object, or concept." Passion hooks our learners into making a commitment to their education each day. The gap between what learners are doing now and what they have potential to accomplish if passion were a part of the equation is what we call the Passion Gap. The Passion Gap is dangerous for everyone—from burning out our talented and gifted students to ignoring the ones in the middle to alienating and ostracizing those with behavioral, cognitive, or other challenges. Worst of all is having students who just plain give up.

We are losing millions of students and teachers in this gap. They are falling hard and fast. Learners like first-grader, Houston, is just beginning to fall:

Houston is passionate about trucks, cars, and super heroes, struggles a bit with reading, and has an average I.Q. Interestingly, he barely meets minimum requirements for first grade. He comes to school and plays the game. He sits through calendar time getting the big idea that it's about the days of the week, counting and patterns, yet the truth is he really doesn't care. He thinks, "What's the big deal? It's Wednesday. I can look at the calendar myself. The teacher-lady will tell me what day it is anyway." He goes through the motions of "sounding-out" the short vowels and reading the guided book of the week, Dan Can Fan his Tan Can. He memorizes the code, yet scores in the lower middle stanine on his developmental assessment. Next, the students are directed to follow the usual writing routine: Write your name first, then copy and respond to the writing prompt of the day. Today's prompt reads, "The best thing ever about school is..." Houston gets excited and draws a picture of a car. He thinks it's the best writing work he's completed so far this year. He thinks, "Finally, something I'm interested in and know a lot about!" Proud of his work, he hopes to publish it in his classroom library. He writes his rendition of the prompt at the top, "The first car I ever made." Remembering that he was supposed to write his name first, he draws an arrow from his name to the beginning of his writing. He gets his paper back, a couple days later with the directions to do it over, this time, following the directions. Houston is confused. He did the best diagram with the best writing ever, and he didn't do it right. And this happens again and again, day after day, until his passion for learning is lost.

Fast forward, Houston age 15, now a high sophomore:

He appears to be the model student. He gets his assignments done on time, earns good grades and receives few complaints from his teachers concerning inappropriate behavior and attitude. It has been years, however, since learning excited and made sense to him. Now, he's going through the motions of school. He doesn't connect with what he is learning and sees little reason for why he must know it. Houston has become an endangered learner indeed.

His family shared this story with us:

Houston was laying on the living room couch with a book over his face. As evidenced by the pile of sticky notes, empty soda cans, and scattered wrappers, he had been studying for some time. Mom asked him about what he was studying. He pulled the book down from over his eyes and reluctantly replied, "It's, um, biology or somethin'." As he sits up and flips the book back open, grabs his highlighter, and with a role of his eyes says to her: "I gotta take this course. I don't know why...." Then he says the very words no teacher (his mom happened to be a teacher) ever wants to hear: "This sucks! School sucks! I'LL NEVER USE THIS STUFF ANYWAY. Why does it even matter?" and he continues on his work.

Houston's story illustrates that the problem we face with student achievement goes far deeper than frustration or lack of motivation, and way beyond simple boredom. Students are not falling though the cracks because our standards are low, or because our classrooms are ill equipped with the latest technology, or because we failed to use the right book or strategy. They are falling because we have not yet found a way to sustain the energy, excitement, and love for learning they came with when they first entered our classrooms.

In the preface to this book, we introduced you to our young friend, Haley. We're confident that each and every day, thousands of little "Haley's" run to school! They are excited, inquisitive, and on fire to learn. For most young learners and students, there are not enough hours in the day to quench their insatiable curiosity or satisfy their need to know more. Yet, by the time they reach secondary education, enthusiasm, engagement, and love for learning is at an all-time low.

What is learning like at your school? How many learners like Haley are present, actively engaged, and interested in the texts and topics they are exploring? More important, how many students are passionate about their learning?

Minding the Passion Gap

Finding our way out of the gap is possible, and it will be the little steps we take that will make the most difference. It is our attention to detail that arms us in this fight. What will matter most is how we respond to the first roll of the eyes, the heads on the desks, and how our ears perk up at the first whispers of, "Do we really need to know this stuff?" The potential for teachers and schools to remain relevant and powerful forces in children's lives is enormous, but it is critical that we are clearly aligned in our values, words, and behaviors. What types of behaviors are rewarded by our schools and in our classrooms and what types are "punished"? What will we do to address this gap between what we say we want, and what we actually do in our classrooms?

We start by recognizing and admitting when we are disconnected from our students. To help illustrate what we mean by recognizing when we are creating a gap, we introduce you to key research by Westby and Dawson (1995). They studied the characteristics of creative and noncreative students, then asked teachers to rate their favorite and least favorite students based on those traits.

First, teachers were asked if they valued joy, creativity, and working with passionate students. They overwhelmingly answered "Yes!" Next, they were asked to look at their own students and rate them on a variety of traits, ranging from highly creative, such as being determined, independent, individualistic, impulsive, and likely to take risks, to traits that are associated with low levels of creativity, such as peaceable, reliable, tolerant, steady, and practical. After they rated their students on these traits, they were asked to rate them from their least favorite to most favorite students.

Interestingly, there was a significant negative correlation between the degree of passion of the student and his favorable teacher rating. In essence, there was a passion gap. The most creative and passionate students were the least favorite of the teachers across the entire sample surveyed. Additionally, the students who were rated as favorites possessed traits that would seem counter-productive to creative behavior like conformity and the unquestioning acceptance of authority.

The passion gap has been around and recognized for some time now. Feldhusen and Treffinger (1975) concluded that 96% of teachers reported that creativity should be promoted in the classroom. However, when asked which students they actually preferred to teach, teachers chose the students who were most compliant. These studies confirm what we suspect: What we claim to want and what we actually reward in practice are two very different things.

We are all guilty in preferring compliance when we admit that we favor the following student behaviors:

♦ Raising hands to speak

♦ Answering our questions

♦ Following the directions on assignments

♦ Filling in our blanks

♦ Pursuing topics we deem important

However, Ken Kay, president of the Partnership for 21st Century Skills (2008), states that we need our students to be:

- Adaptable

- Flexible

- Creative

- Innovative

- Leaders

- Cross-cultural

This is the skill set that has been the subject of countless national and international discussions and research initiatives (The Partnership for 21st Century Skills, 2008). The skill set that we consider to be key in enabling American students and companies to differentiate themselves from others across the globe is the very skill set most at risk within our schools. Including passion in our objectives is the only way these 21st century skills can be taught and outcomes be met. If we study those who embody this "new skill set" across any discipline, field, or domain, we will discover that a fierce passion is at the foundation of their work and accomplishment. It was the passion that Michael Jordan possessed for the game that fueled him to practice in the way that he did. It was how Albert Einstein passionately pursued his questions about the world that led him to the theories that changed it. It will be the passion that students hold, not for every school subject, but for the ACT and PRIVILEGE of learning that will allow them to reach rigorous outcomes and excellence.

How do we put this into practice? Is this too much to ask? Let us clearly state that we are not giving up our expectations for classroom management and for appropriate, respectful behavior. On the contrary, we know that including passion as part of our teaching mindset will take care of many of these issues. We are advocating that we need both the outcomes we seek as well as the 21st century skills in the teaching equation, and we can have both through the Learning Clubs framework in the Clubhouse Classroom. Before we delve into the nuts and bolts of setting up a Clubhouse Classroom, we must first address how to close the passion gap.

Closing the Gap

We stated earlier that one of the first steps in closing the gap is recognizing when we are disconnected from our students and admitting it. The next step is taking action. Parker Palmer, in his text *The Courage to Teach* (1998), moves us into taking action: "We can, whenever and wherever we choose, successfully teach all children whose schooling is of interest to us. We already know more than we need to know in order to do that. But what we are missing right now is the will, the passion, and the courage to actually do and make those kind of changes that will render young people successful" (p. 173).

Palmer reminds us that we know more today about how people learn than at any other time in history. Closing the passion gap is possible when we remember "the people" in the learning equation. This will be accomplished by understanding what passion is, what passion can do, where it comes from, and how to make it a part of learning—putting passion into practice.

What does putting passion into practice look like? In the chapters ahead, we will answer this in detail across grade levels and content areas. All learners can reach a new level of scholarship and engagement when we commit to these three simple truths:

- ♦ Know and Show Your Passion
- ♦ Know and Show the Students' Passion
- ♦ Know and Show the World Passion

Step One: Know and Show Your Passion

Douglas Kaufman (2002) says it well: "If I want my students to be passionately literate people, I, too, must be a passionate person who reads, writes, and learns in front of them" (p. 51). When we are joyful, amazing things happen. When we shared Houston's story at a recent conference (ironically at a session for educators interested in transforming education), a participant in the audience said what many of us have thought at one time in our careers, "That's too bad, but the reality is that school isn't always interesting, and our kids have to learn to deal with it. After all, how is it possible to make something like trigonometry or physics passionate?"

Professor Richard Marin whole-heartedly agrees (as, we believe, would most practicing scientists and mathematicians). Listen in to journalist Anna Neumann's interview (2009) with Dr. Marin as he describes the world of subatomic quantum mechanics and microphysics for us:

> I think physics is much more of an addiction than a choice of career. Physics is part of such a large fabric to me. When I was deciding what field to choose over twenty years ago, I had a dilemma between philosophy and mathematics and physics. Those are the things I was drawn to. And I never separate them in my mind, even though I've chosen to be a physicist.

Physics is something that addresses what it means to be human. I think physics, like any truly analytical discipline, is a study of the human mind. It's the study of what it means to be who you are. It's a study of your own person. And so by looking out there, I'm looking in here. And physics, to me, is an unbelievably precise and efficient and beautiful—incredibly beautiful—way of studying myself. And of studying other humans. To me, that's what it's all about.

I'm not so sure how common this is, but when things are going well, what happens is first of all, it affects me physically, not just intellectually. My body kicks into a higher gear. I shake, and I can't stop moving. I barely sleep as it is, and I sleep even less. Although it might sound like it's distracting, it's not. It's wonderful, it really is. My students say that I start spewing forth conjectures or mathematical ideas without really knowing where they're coming from. I just love when I get these feelings that I'm not creating physics or mathematics, but it's being revealed to me. And so this revelatory experience is certainly a part of the great times. That's something I really, really, really enjoy. Where suddenly you come across a thought that you didn't know you had—a really startling experience.

"Exhilarated," "Excited," "Beautiful," "Addictive," and "Wonderful" are not words that immediately come to mind when describing our physics class in high school, but after a class or two with Professor Marin, who wouldn't see physics differently?

Douglas Reeves (2010) tells us from his infinite wisdom and research on what really matters in student achievement is that "it is practices and people, not programs, that make the difference" (p. 3). We must remember the people factor, and the teacher makes all the difference. A teacher's passion is just as critical as student passion. It is incredibly contagious in the learning process, making even a macro-molecule something we would attend to and care about. When the teacher has a high level of passion for the material, it makes the information come alive and stirs interest and motivation. When a passionate teacher connects the material to something the student is passionate about, the teaching is inspirational. Instead of trying to motivate our students to learn, we are inspiring our students to learn.

Let students see your passion. Let them see your commitment to your topic, your loves, and how pursuing that passion changed the way you see the world.

Step Two: Know and Show the Students' Passion

As we have seen, kids don't need us to make them passionate. They are born that way. They do need us to help them STAY that way, and to help them to USE that passion in important and productive ways. Students will become MORE passionate about learning and school when they believe you value their passion and back that up with teacher modeling and action. We have learners waiting to have their passions discovered and rekindled, and it will take your courage and commitment to be the teacher who helps them find it.

The best example of teacher passion put into practice is teacher and professor, Donald Graves (2003, p. 74), a master at connecting his passion for writing with individual student passion. He showed us how to teach our young writers to write about what they know and care about, by sharing what we know and care about. He taught us to ask our students about their interests and how to use these passions to drive writing instruction. He reminds us to ask ourselves and reflect as teachers about these simple questions:

+ Who walks through our door each day?

+ Who are they?

+ What do they value?

+ What is important to them?

Our current school model, however, leaves the learner out of the conversation and often confirms the perceptions that we are not listening, that we do not value their opinions and talents, and that their passion is not important because it doesn't fit into the schedule or curriculum.

To find answers to these questions, we must start by pulling students into the learning conversation. We, the authors, have been so fortunate to have had opportunities to ask these questions across schools, grade levels, and a wide variety of educational settings. Hundreds of students shared with us exactly what it would take for them to not only learn, but to be competent, empowered, and passionate enough to continue the pursuit throughout their lives. The following describes our passion conversations with these learners.

We begin the passion and learning conversation with one of our favorite books, *Through the Cracks* (1994) by Carolyn Sollman, Barbara Emmons, and Judith Paolini. It tells the story of two disengaged students literally falling through the cracks of their classroom. The endangered learners are saved by the courage and heroism of brave teachers who lead them toward learning that is personalized, meaningful, and real.

After reading the story, we have students examine the classes where they feel like they are falling. Students are guided to talk or write about the conditions in which learning happens best for them rather than their likes or dislikes for specific teachers. They think and then complete these statements:

♦ I learn best when…

♦ I am most excited when my teachers let me…

♦ I appreciate my teacher when…

♦ I am motivated by…

♦ I am happiest when…

Here are the responses from a kindergarten girl, age 6:

Student: I learn best when: "At math because we learn…we learn how to count to 100."
I am most excited when my teachers let me: "Have a surprise!"

Teacher: Tell me more about that…

Student: "You let us have free time and play at the art center!"
I appreciate (like) my teacher when: "You let us have surprises."
I am motivated by *(I try my best when)*: "We do spelling."
I am happiest when: "We go swimming because it's fun and because you can jump in the water."

The teacher goes further by sharing an example of her own passionate learning experience. Here's a snippet of what that conversation leads to:

Teacher: Boys and Girls, Think about a time in your learning where you felt so good, so excited, so on fire, that you did not want to stop! You know the kind that makes you want to say—"This rocks!" (Feel free to pick your own two words!)

I want to share with you when that happened for me. While I am describing that learning experience, I would like you to think about a few things. I want you to understand how exciting this was for me, and how much learning like this matters. But more important, I want you to be thinking about the ways your learning experience was similar.

I remember the moment I became a writer. It was during my 5th grade year, and my teacher's name was Mr. Nester.

He allowed time every day to write what we wanted to write about. I had never had a teacher like this ever before.

I can remember asking him if I could take stacks of paper home so that I could continue the stories I started at school. The more time I had to write, the more I thought about my writing, and the more I wanted to write. As each day passed, I started to feel like a writer.

Without the gifts of time and consistency, I am not sure that would have happened.

Here's why that is important. My goal is to try to discover with you how learning like this happens. If we can find out what it takes for learners to feel like saying "THIS ROCKS!" or "WOW-THAT WAS AMAZING!," then we can work to create experiences for this to happen more often. Good idea?

After modeling our own learning stories, we ask students to describe their passionate learning experience to a partner or small group. We use the following questions to guide the dialogue:

What got you excited about the learning/study?

♦ When did you realize that you were really "into" it?

♦ What was the payoff for you? What made you want to keep going?

♦ What do you remember most?

Students spent 30 minutes digging into their memories, sharing stories, and prodding each other with questions. Here is an example from a boy, age 12.

"My experience is about baseball. What got me excited about it? When I got better, I started liking it more. When did I realize I was really into it? When you're having fun and doing good it feels like you want to keep playing because you're not failing all the time. I like it because I am good. What is my payoff ? I feel that if I keep practicing I'll play on a better team, like an all-star team. What do I remember most? I've had lots of moments. When we went through the line-up twice, I think three times against this really good team and we beat them 18–0. It was BEAST (kid-slang for great)."

When we brought our conversations back to the whole group, we listened to each other with excitement and attention. The stories were fascinating and rang true, prompting us to piggyback on each other's tales. They were exactly what we needed to create a crystal-clear focus on what passion-driven learning looks like.

We asked the students to return to their learning stories and consider their experience beyond the initial excitement and energies they felt at the start. We wanted them to understand that passionate learning is more than a fleeting moment of motivation and excitement. We explained to students that passion-driven learning involves more than liking what you do or the project you are working on. Passion is present when you have a willingness to attend to the work when it's not so fun. Passion is present in your learning when you are willing to persevere across the obstacles you face in order to succeed at the learning. Does the learning you describe have attributes of courage, perseverance, tenacity, and a "whatever it takes" feel to it? Consider the age and grade level of your students to determine how to complete the interviews. More independent students can complete this in small groups of three to four or in pairs. The teacher can interview younger or less independent learners. The teacher can schedule three interviews a day at independent work time to truly get to know their students. We used the following questions to help them dig deeper into their learning stories:

♦ Is this learning you described something you would be willing to continue?

♦ How do you know you could/would to "stick-with-it" or continue the study for long periods of time?

♦ What would happen when/if you encounter a challenge?

♦ How do you handle "hard"?

♦ What/who helps you get past the obstacles?

♦ What would make you want to quit?

Their stories helped us crystallize what makes them feel prepared, confident, and ready for the world and put us in touch with the individuals we teach. These conversations have the potential to transform the state of teaching and learning, if we are willing to take time and listen.

Step Three: Know and Show the World Passion

We are inundated with research and evidence of how the world has changed, that learners are different now, and that the jobs of the future are waiting to be created. Preparing students, workers, and citizens to be successful in this unpredictable global society is a challenge of immense proportion.

Our children must compete for jobs with increasingly well-educated young people from around the world. The jobs they hold will demand new skills, familiarity with new technologies, and an understanding of their roles in a larger environment. But have we told and taught our students that the world and the workforce will demand their passion?

Peruse any current issue of a prominent business magazine: *Forbes, Fast Company, Business Week,* or *Inc.,* and you will find an open and directive dialogue about passion as not only the fundamental success factor but an essential economic and competitive advantage for individuals and organizations wishing to stay relevant and viable. The hunt for game-changing stars is intense. Competitors in every industry are in a race to sign up the right people and turn them loose on winning projects. Companies and organizations are beginning to recognize and prioritize passion over protocol. They will ask for more than grade-point averages and I.Q.; they will also ask for what journalist and author, Thomas Friedman (*The World is Flat,* 2008) refers to as the passion quotient (P.Q.). He argues that passion for something is more important than I.Q. Workers with P.Q. thrive in the world today and will continue to thrive in the future.

Will our students stand out? Can they survive and adapt through change? Do they consider themselves to be passionate? Will they describe their talents to others and promote themselves as the "one for the job"? Will others characterize them as a standout because of their passion?

If we haven't made a strong enough case yet for passion, we share these words:

> Somewhere in America there's an entrepreneur seeking a loan to start a business that could transform an industry—but she hasn't secured it yet. There's a researcher with an idea for an experiment that might offer a new cancer treatment—but he hasn't found the funding yet. There's a child with an inquisitive mind staring up at the night sky. And maybe she has the potential to change our world—but she doesn't know it yet…
>
> As you know, scientific discovery takes far more than the occasional flash of brilliance—as important as that can be. Usually, it takes time and hard work and patience; it takes training; it requires the support of a nation. But it holds a promise like no other area of human endeavor…
>
> America's young people will rise to the challenge if given the opportunity—if called upon to join a cause larger than themselves. We have evidence. The average age in NASA's

mission control during the Apollo 17 mission was just 26. We know that young people today are just as ready to tackle the grand challenges of this century. Who will ignite the desire to learn in the adults today so they will ignite the desire to learn in our children tomorrow?

This was President of the United States Barack Obama speaking at the 2009 Annual Meeting of National Academy of Sciences. In closing, the president issued a renewed commitment to education and challenged all educators to bring passion into the classroom, to:

♦ use their love and knowledge of their content area to spark the same sense of wonder and excitement in a new generation...

♦ spend time in the classroom, talking and showing young people what it is that your work can mean, and what it means to you...

♦ participate in programs to allow students to get a degree in science fields and a teaching certificate at the same time...

♦ participate in new and creative ways to engage young people to create and build and invent—to be makers of things, not just consumers of things

And to that, we say within a resounding, Yes, We will. We will. We will. Let's start that conversation now!

2

Let's Talk About Passion

Develop a passion for learning. If you do, you will never cease to grow.

—Anthony J. D'Angelo

Whatever subject we teach or position we hold, how we talk shapes how we think and act in that work. Our language defines and determines the interactions and attitudes we will ultimately associate with the content and the process. Our conversations become our culture. We propose that if we truly want to change the organization, we need to change the talk happening within it.

Consider this:

♦ How openly do we talk about passion?

♦ How comfortable are we using the word "passion"? With colleagues? With our students?

♦ How often does passion occur during teaching and learning?

Our goal in this chapter is to get you comfortable with the word "passion" and to help you find a way to define it for yourself and your students. This is more than a simple exercise in semantics. As educators, we have been given the distinction of being a passionate profession, and it is our duty to craft those perceptions about how passion fits into our work. If we don't, others will do it for us, and the result may not be to our liking.

As we begin, we have some questions to help guide you through this chapter and eventually, to the acceptance of this "P" word. Take a few minutes and think about what passion means to you. When you say the word, what is the first thing you see? Hear? Feel? Now, put your mind's eye in the heads and hearts of your students. When they hear the word "passion," what emotions and senses do they experience?

Defining Passion

Passion is not only a powerful word, it is a popular one, yielding over 150 million hits on a basic Google Search. Digging into those queries, canvassing the literature and the research, we quickly discovered that there are about as many meanings for the word "passion" as there are people taking up the question: What is passion and why does it matter?

The impending trend in much of the world's perceptions and opinions of passion are superficial, frivolous, and simple. With images of mountains moving and feelings of volcanoes erupting, it is easy to understand why passion is often considered a lavish concept, something only possessed and embodied by extremely high-energy, extravagant people and associated with endeavors that yield significant emotion, response, and achievements. After teasing out some of the historical meanings of the word, however, we found these sentiments indicate a flawed concept of passion, its place in the classroom, and its purpose in the educational process.

Passion comes from the Latin word "patior," meaning to suffer or to endure. In its origin, passion is used to describe someone who willingly opens up to suffering and finds fulfillment therein. It properly describes the final days of the life of Christ. We are familiar with the expression, "The PASSION of Christ," yet brutal crippling pain is not often the first thing that pops to mind.

As we talked to fellow educators and teachers about their definitions, they had plenty to add:

♦ Passion is pure JOY.

♦ Passion is focused consciousness that changes worlds.

♦ Passion is my work.

♦ Passion is contagious.

♦ Passion is devotion with enthusiasm.

♦ Passion is attractive. When you see it, hear, it—you just want some of it.

♦ Passion is timeless, it can't be shaken from you and is what you live for.

♦ Passion is energy with intent and purpose.

♦ Passion is the engine that powers life.

♦ Passion is an intense feeling for life, people, and everything else you believe in and love.

♦ Passion is desperately needed but doesn't come from a "program."

- Passion takes time, but the reward is sweet.

- Passion enables us to overcome obstacles (both real and imagined) and to see the world as a place of infinite potential.

- Passion is living your life doing what you love.

- Passion is WAAAYYYY better than Discipline!!

- Passion is gusto.

- Passion is disruptive excitement.

- Passion is when our hearts embrace our thoughts.

These statements leave us with a much deeper and much clearer image of what Passion is and what Passion is not:

Passion Is NOT	Passion IS
◆ Crazy or wacky ◆ Something that can be done to someone ◆ A replacement for hard work ◆ Always a grand celebration ◆ Easy or always comfortable ◆ Random	◆ Serious ◆ Internal ◆ Persevering ◆ Often quiet ◆ Difficult and rebellious at times ◆ Purposeful

In order to tap into passion as a resource to motivate, engage, and empower our learners, we must understand these underlying values of passion. Passion is not one thing. It is more than a unitary skill or competency that can be trained or cultivated by and of itself. We find it more useful to summarize the distinctive attributes, behaviors, and ideas associated with passion.

P.A.S.S.I.O.N.

To support this understanding, we have created the acronym PASSION to summarize the intrinsic nature and architecture of work and individuals driven by passion. This provides us with both the language and actions needed to create a classroom culture that is passion-driven. Feel free to adapt and change as needed:

PASSION IS

P erseverance

A ction driven

S trength building

S ustainable

I nquisitive

O wnership

N ever-ending

P–Passion is Perseverance.

The Latin origin of the word comes from "passio," or suffering. Suffering pain is a very real part of it and one of the reasons many people are not willing to expose themselves to it. Passionate learners combine fun, playfulness, and discipline and, at that same time, accept the necessity for endurance and perseverance.

A–Passion is Action Oriented.

It is not passive. It is about pursuit. People with passion are driven to pursue and create. They may read books and observe others, but they are not content as bystanders. They feel an overwhelming urge to engage, to experience, and to test their own capabilities.

Passion often grows again once action is taken. Passionate action begets passionate action. Remember the first time you practiced a new activity? The more you learn and experience, the more interested and passionate you became.

S–Passion is Strength-Building.

Eliciting deep passions requires strength. We have learned well from school to keep this side of ourselves hidden. It sometimes takes enormous strength and willpower to overcome obstacles, but passion gives us strength to continue forward. Passionate people are at the same time humble. These individuals know that they sometimes stand on the shoulders of giants who preceded them and acknowledge the contributions that have inspired them. They gain strength from the example of others.

S–Passion is Sustainable.

It is endurance with an edge of obsession. It drives the athlete to practice thousands of hours or a performer to rehearse to the point of physical and mental exhaustion. Passionate writers seem to sweat blood. They don't always want to sit down and write, but feel compelled to do so.

I–Passion is Inquiry.

Passionate learners not only ask a lot of questions, they have developed a questioning disposition. When we train students to believe that everything can be neatly answered, passion is deterred. But when passion fuels new and better questions, students' muscles of inquiry are stronger. They tolerate not knowing the answer, yet feel the inner need to find it.

O–Passion is Ownership.

Passion says, "I believe in this. I own this. I think about it even when I'm not on the clock. I know we can do this better than anyone else can." This sense of ownership becomes a responsibility—the mission to pursue excellent work.

N–Passion is Never Ending.

Proficiency is never achieved when you are passionate about something. It is a lifelong pursuit. Passion may sleep, but it never dies.

So let's talk about passion, now. When you say the word "passion," what is the first thing you see? Hear? Feel? How have your ideas changed? Put your mind's eye in the heads and hearts of your students, when they hear the word, what will they be thinking of and doing? Does it match what you want them to be thinking and doing? We hope that we have given you a clearer image and understanding of what passion is and the language to use when asserting it and including passion into our conversations. We may not control the standards, the curriculum, or even the lesson we have to teach on Monday morning, but we do control the talk. Making passion a part of our language changes us. It changes our thoughts, our attitudes, and our behaviors and by simply changing the conversation, we change the culture.

Passion-Driven Learning

We conclude our talk about the word "passion" with a formula that illustrates the connection between student engagement and passion-driven learning. When manipulating each of the two variables, you can either increase or decrease a student's level of learning engagement.

Engagement is a function of the learner's relationship with two things:

1. WHAT students are learning: the content, text, and topics they may be studying

2. WHERE (and with whom) the learning takes place: in the classroom, the environment, and the context

Engagement = What + Where

We know that engagement matters. We know how to change the "WHAT" by providing students new and different things to learn. We can give them a different book, update the lesson plan, or allow them to explore a new and more interesting topic, and most likely we will see an increase in student engagement and participation. We have also made great strides in altering the WHERE. We can rearrange our classrooms to become more inviting, spruce up our lesson delivery, and present ideas in enlivening contexts like field trips or through demonstrations. We have executed this formula with some success by making what students "do" in school more exciting and hands-on, and more related to the real world—and by making our classroom environments better places to "do" it in now. We conclude with confidence that changing the "what" and "where" improves student engagement.

Now see what happens when we add passion into the formula. Who we are adds a whole different layer, and it has everything to do with learning. Noted educator and researcher Alfie Kohn has studied motivation and engagement theory extensively. His excellent book *Punished by Rewards* (1993) reminds us that passion is better than manufactured fun. Understanding who we are and how we feel significantly influences how we learn, more so than the content or the environment. Our passion moves us deeper. In this sense, learning driven by passion functions like a love that endures for a long time. Outside events and contexts impact our learning, but passion-driven learning is not ultimately determined by or easily swayed by the external factors. Although we do not want to take all the "romance" out of it, we can express passion-driven learning in another formula:

Passion-Driven Learning = What + Where + WHO

WHO we are as learners is influenced by the outside. We all have memories of those special classes and teachers who made learning extraordinary; like Mr. Nestor, the teacher that allowed writing to happen every day.

Yet, the truly defining moments in learning are those that occur on the inside, making WHO we are the ultimate contributor to learning success. Our attitudes, beliefs, expectations, and knowledge are shaped by those experiences in positive and negative ways. Who we are determines the energy and effort we are willing to put into the job and the enthusiasm with which we approach the work. Truly passionate learners are more than excited about learning. They operate with an unwavering confidence and strength. They not only act differently, they see themselves and learning differently.

In an effort to paint a clearer picture of what those differences entail, we asked 400 teachers to identify and describe the most passionate learners in their classrooms. Across age and grade, traits and attributes, they create a profile of the learner we are seeking to understand and develop. Passionate learners are:

- Fiercely driven
- Determined to be excellent
- Introspective
- Open-minded
- Challenged to discover
- Self-directed
- Actively involved
- Self-aware
- Adaptable
- Perceptive
- Reflective
- Flexible
- Willing to risk
- Courageous
- Dedicated
- Problem solvers
- Unconcerned with impressing others
- Conscientious in convictions

Learners with these attributes can learn under ANY circumstance and can sustain themselves under difficult conditions.

Does passion guarantee successful learning? There are no guarantees in learning or in life. The fact remains that no one can predict with certainty what lies ahead for our learners in the next decade, the next year, or even in the next week. What we can claim with certainty is this: With passion in the learning equation, we have a much better shot at meeting those challenges, achieving those goals, and creating much happier individuals in the process of doing both.

What Passion Can Do

And just to summarize what passion CAN do and its benefits, let's review:

Passion...

- **Creates a Sense of Urgency.** There is a sense of urgency when we feel passionate about something. This urgency is the enemy of apathy, complacency, and procrastination. The goal becomes too important to let anything get in the way.

- **Provides Focus.** When we feel passionate about something, passion provides us with an unequaled source of energy and enables us to survive setbacks and challenges.

- **Ignites Curiosity.** Champion learners are curious about everything. They ask questions and get themselves involved in all stages of learning, without worrying about the answer, but relishing the process. They have learned that by posing questions, they can generate interest and aliveness in the most exciting or mundane situation. This inquisitive attitude fuels their unrelenting quest for continuous learning.

- **Promotes Innovation.** Think about how students in your classes are able to demonstrate originality and inventiveness in their work; the fuel for their creativity and problem solving is the passion they feel for their idea or topic.

- **Supports Collaboration.** Although passion is typically addressed as an individual trait, successful learners understand the critical importance of the team. Passionate people find ways to connect with others by laying the perfect groundwork to demonstrate their ability to work effectively with diverse teams; to be flexible and helpful to accomplish a common goal; and to assume shared responsibility for collaborative work.

- **Raises the Standard.** Think of an important project you have been involved in. Evaluating information for its accuracy and clarity is critically important to the work. As students understand these high-level skills, they will struggle to think more critically about messages and points of view and to competently convey messages that can influence beliefs and behaviors.

- **Encourages Accountability.** Passionate people have a tendency to hold others accountable and tolerate nothing less than the full-blown commitment of everyone around them. They are not afraid to ask the tough questions and call out those that fail to hold up their end of the task. Their commitment to a higher standard becomes contagious, spreads throughout the entire system or project, and eventually becomes the standard that all are accustomed to.

♦ **Allows Us To Be Courageous**. Learning is a high-risk endeavor. It takes courage to try something new that you can't yet do, or to practice something you are not good at, especially when others, who may be more experienced or more developed in that skill, surround you. It takes courage and passion to stand upon your convictions. Passion helps people deal with the fear of change, criticism, and failure. Stepping out of your comfort zone and risking more becomes easier as the passion intensifies.

♦ **Provides Us with Energy.** There is less external discipline, less apathy, and absenteeism in a passionate work environment where meaningful work and a heroic cause energize people. People don't want to miss the thrill of the journey and the significant things going on at work.

♦ **Becomes Contagious**. Perhaps the most exciting benefit that comes from cultivating passion is the enthusiasm it generates. Passionate people inspire hope and enthusiasm. That's why they're so attractive to be around. There's an intensity, a commitment, a PASSION with which they approach their work—it's inviting, tantalizing, alluring, and inspiring all wrapped up in the same package.

Does passion guarantee learning? You decide.

3

Clubhouse Learning: Where Passion Meets Practice

Coming together is a beginning.
Keeping together is progress.
Working together is success.

—Henry Ford

Walk into a Passion-Driven Clubhouse Classroom and you will see writing, blogging, sketching, and labeling of learning that students and teacher have encountered in the past 24 hours. We call this part of the daily Opening Message, "Learning Now!" Students are instructed to search for new or interesting information and have it ready for the Boardroom meeting. After this, you will see them gathered in Learning Club groups until the Boardroom meeting is conducted. Even though this routine is labeled the Opening Message, the routine is geared to sharing current or past learning. Perhaps it is something interesting and important a student has learned about world history while working in one of the Learning Clubs. Or, it could be an awareness of an important current event, for example, the number of earthquakes occurring around the world and the possible implications.

Next, you will hear the teacher, the Chief Learning Officer or C.L.O., call to order the daily Boardroom meeting. Plans are made and discussions are held pertaining to the day's work in Learning Clubs and content area instruction. Students are dismissed from the Boardroom, and a day of both independent and interdependent learning is unleashed.

How did we get to this place of empowered, engaged, and passionate learning? We've replicated something that we've known for a long time. Let us return to childhood. Perhaps yours is similar to ours.

Our Very First Learning Club

Our first learning club was founded in the summer we were seven. Everyone in the neighborhood belonged. We each had a role of some sort. We acted like presidents, treasurers, and secretaries. Dues were paid in bubble gum and Kevin Franklin's mom made great chocolate chip cookies, and the neighbor lady, Mrs. Weasley, liked to give us Swiss cheese for payment of good deeds. Outside of the classroom, our research and investigation led us on magnificent adventures. We discovered the thrill and pitfalls of entrepreneurialism and understood the value of marketing as our lemonade stand gained popularity or fell short. We were inventors and explorers as we found new ways to have fun and combat boredom on those long summer days. We took the hard knocks as citizen journalists who were too quick to reveal their "sources." We read and we wrote, we told fantastic stories, and we learned a lot. We learned about the world, how to get along and got to know ourselves—and we did it together in our very first learning club.

These experiences taught us unique ways of knowing and reminded us that we do our best learning when we research topics and issues that matter deeply to us. We are smarter and stronger when we do it in the presence of others. The Learning Club structure that we so fondly remember as beginning readers, writers, and researchers mirrors the vision we have for learning today. This chapter introduces you to the philosophy and thinking behind the Clubhouse Classroom. Later, in the next chapter, we show you how to launch the learning through the Learning Clubs framework and what it actually looks like from day one.

The Philosophy:
Clubs Are Passion Playing Fields

As adults, we still enjoy the experience of participating in a club. Clubs exist for just about everything. Do you want to expand your cooking skills or become a better tennis player? Clubs draw people to them. You can join a club to learn a new skill and find people with similar hobbies and interests. Clubs are enticing because they help us improve our passions. Some clubs are informal. Perhaps you have a little coffee club, made up of a select group of like-minded friends that you meet with to solve America's educational dilemmas. Maybe you have a club of buddies who gather religiously for Monday night football. Other clubs are formal, like a tennis club, for instance.

Members have varying levels of skill, yet everyone is committed to the club. They pay their dues to reap the club's specialized benefits. The members may be a mixture of true competitors who keep each other sharp, while others just want their weekly social game of doubles. Others join as beginners in search of lessons and exercise.

Whether it is an informal morning coffee group or a formal club with bylaws, we form clubs because we have a common interest in what the club has to offer. Clubs are serious business whether it's an occasional book club or a scheduled round of golf. These groups require a level of work, skill, socialization, and emotion. The members are motivated to participate because they have a passion for what the club has to offer, and they expect to have some fun.

The beauty of clubs is that they allow us to be both independent and interdependent. We can practice alone, read alone, think alone, then find our group and extend this interest. People are drawn to clubs because they are given a chance to participate with a group of people with common interests. Taking it deeper, the members share a passion for what the club offers. If you goof up and hit your drive into the next fairway, nobody really cares. Your foursome makes some comment about the wind or how to keep your elbow straight. You can take a mulligan, try again, or leave it the way it is. Clubs are social and fun. You are given the opportunity to fail often and make mistakes without getting laughed at. In other words, clubs are "passion playing fields."

What Makes Club Life Enticing?

♦ Clubs are based on interest and passion.

♦ Clubs have both independent and interdependent opportunities for the members.

♦ Clubs provide a community. We have a team of cheerleaders, diverse experts, and peers who are committed to helping us succeed.

♦ Clubs welcome diversity.

♦ Clubs are participatory.

♦ Clubs scaffold: Their supportive, collaborative, and creative environments enable us to clarify our next actions, what strategies to use, and how to most productively proceed.

♦ Clubs are fun! They inspire, energize, and breed confidence.

- Clubs empower: When we consistently connect with other passion-led people, get clarity about our goals, and receive support and accountability around those goals, we are empowered.

What if we took the natural, engaging framework of club life and applied it to our classroom? We would create:

- A community of learners

- Active participants

- Respect for one another

- Opportunities to practice alone

- Time to share together

- Diversity of student knowledge and skills

- Respectful and responsible learners working toward a shared goal, vision, or task!

The clubhouse atmosphere encourages student participation, contribution, and engagement in thinking. Students have time to experience independence, time to practice alone, time to fail, time to reflect, and time to pursue and solve their own problems. They have the chance to learn and work with others and to engage in conversation and dialogue centered on important tasks and projects. Our students' success inside and outside of the classroom depends upon their actions as learners, both as individuals and as a community of learners. We need both "I"s in our classrooms: independence and interdependence.

In the next section, we will visit the valuable lessons of the workshop philosophy of teaching and learning and apply them to the 21st century classroom demands.

The Workshop Classroom: Driven by Curiosity

"I have no special talents. I am only passionately curious."

—Albert Einstein

Each day we model that learning is dynamic. It changes, evolves, and grows. True learning happens when we take action on it. Students discover that learning happens when and if we are able to:

- Find the words to describe it

- Discover strategies to capture and collect it

- Develop research that's changing what's possible, changing our understanding of what can be done

- Discover people who share similar ideas and interests, who are working in similar ways

- Collect images that move us to wonder more—or move us to action

We come back to our one simple goal, one that will follow our learners into their adult lives: We want to teach our students *how* to learn about what *they want* to learn about. We harness the curiosity of our learners and teach them how to use this inquiry efficiently and successfully. Frank Serafini's (2004) description of the workshop philosophy of teaching describes the foundation of inquiry that drives the Clubhouse Classroom. He states that by "Providing choice and ownership in the experiences of the reading workshop, responding to students' contributions, providing time and opportunities for students to read and discuss literature, and creating authentic instructional experiences, we can support the kinds of readers we want exiting our classroom at the end of the year" (p. 5).

We take this thinking and move it into all aspects of the day. The workshop classroom of the 21st century operates as a culture of teaming, innovating, and creating, emulating the philosophy of the reading and writing workshop and extending it through the entire day. In these classrooms, students operate in the world of clubs: where learning is constantly moving. The Clubhouse Classroom blends the elements that make the workshop classroom so powerful and effective, with the same demands our learners will need to meet in the years to come.

Now, let us introduce you to the roles of the Clubhouse Classroom, the workshop classroom of the 21st century—a place where teachers and students are engaged and passionate again.

The Role of the Teacher:
Expert Learner & Passion Practitioner

Up to this point, this text has focused primarily on inspiring the passion within our students, yet our passion as teachers is just as critical. Robert L. Fried in *The Game of School* (2005, p. 1) teaches us, "to be a passionate teacher is to be someone in love with the field of knowledge, deeply stirred by issues and ideas that challenge our world, drawn to the dilemmas and potentials of the young people who come into class each day ..."

Passion has to start with us. This isn't always easy. We've all had our frustrating teaching days. Although we try to keep it together when things may be happening in our lives or the students just aren't making the progress we desire, we can temporarily misplace our passion. We know what it's like in our classrooms on these days. Students sense something is different about us. Our passion, or lack thereof, is contagious in the learning process. When we have a high level of passion in the material, it makes the information and content come alive and stirs the interest of our learners. When we lack passion for the material or have one of our "bad days," it creates disinterested learners.

Let us clearly state that teacher passion doesn't automatically translate into student learning. This passion for the "what" can work to our advantage or backfire. We can have so much passion for our content that we forget the learner. Maybe it's math. When teaching mathematics, perhaps you get absorbed in the logic, patterns, and challenge, and forget who's alongside you. We can be absolutely passionate about our teaching and content, yet we must determinedly resist the urge to want total control of it, as if "we own it." Powerful and passionate learning experiences require a classroom environment that allows them to happen. Several of us who have dabbled in or even adopted the workshop classroom philosophy have experienced letting go to some extent.

Take inspiration from a few of the passion practitioners of our time: Nancie Atwell, Douglas Kaufman, and Regie Routman. The common message from these esteemed researchers is that passion starts with us—the teacher. We unearth these precious gems that seem to have been overlooked by the officialdom. Nancie Atwell (2007, p. 67) reminded us, "When teachers demonstrate passion for our fields, we invite students to believe that learning is worthwhile." Douglas Kaufman (2002, July) professes, "...if I want my students to become passionately literate people, I, too, must be a passionate, literate person, who reads, writes, and learns in front of them". Regie Routman oozes passion for learning and models what we must do to show our passion to the learner in her books *Reading Essentials* (2002) and *Literacy at the Crossroads* (1996).

To illustrate, let's visit Mrs. Smith's passion (teacher)-driven classroom. Lesson planning looks different in Mrs. Smith's workshop as she focuses on guiding her students in reaching higher levels of thinking. Rather than simply covering material, students are encouraged to problem-solve and talk to one another. Students engage in dialogue with each other and Mrs. Smith. As the Chief Learning Officer (C.L.O), Mrs. Smith sets the scene for Learning

Club work in a daily meeting time called the "Boardroom Meeting." Mrs. Smith isn't the know-it-all, however, she is the "Expert Learner," and shares what she is currently interested in and how she does her best thinking. She collaborates with the students as learners, not just modeling, but demonstrating her real passion for learning.

In the Clubhouse Classroom, rather than the teacher acting as the classroom Expert, the teacher is the classroom Expert Learner. Take note of this change in mindset from the teacher as the expert "sage on the stage" to a teacher as the Expert Learner and Passionate Practitioner, alongside students engaging in meaningful authentic work in their Learning Clubs.

We invite you to be one of these passion practitioners. The next chapter illustrates how you can model, share, and guide the instruction as Chief Learning Officer. Now, let's look at the role of students in the Clubhouse Classroom.

The Role of the Student: Apprentice Learner and Global Citizen

Years ago, John Dewey taught us that "The essence of the demand for freedom is the need of conditions which will enable an individual to make his own special contribution to a group interest, and to partake of its activities in such ways that social guidance shall be a matter of his own mental attitude, and not a mere authoritative dictation of his acts" (*Democracy and Education*, 1944, p. 444).

Today, Tony Wagner points us back in the direction of the learner in his groundbreaking text, *The Global Achievement Gap* (2008, p. 26–29), stating that, "Working in teams is the way the world works now." Teams are required in order for students to do their best work in the 21st century learning environment. The Clubhouse Classroom gets to the craft of learning needed in our students' futures, and this craft is all about individual contributions in an environment of groups and teamwork.

Google the words *craft* and *education* and you are likely to get craft projects for students. Although the familiar arts and craft work of coloring, cutting, and pasting does have value, craftmanship is also naturally associated with creative endeavor, from potters to basket weavers to artists such as Picasso and Monet. and so we see value in studying their work as master craftsman. Further, their work, more often than not, begins with an apprenticeship. The learner works side by side with an expert, as a team, living the work of the craft. In other words, craft is what we see, hear, read, taste, and feel about creativity. It's the "Do" of creativity. Craft is the vehicle of personal expression and innovation. Machines can't demonstrate craftsmanship. If machines produce high-quality objects, it's the result of fine machining by the innovative humans who created the process and also the result of teamwork and apprenticeship.

Coupled with the concept of student as an apprentice, learning a craft by working as a team member, the Clubhouse Classroom student is also contributing his or talents for the greater good, as a global citizen who is recognized and respected by others, by the community, for passion and special areas of expertise.

The Resident Expert Wall

In the Clubhouse Classroom, students form an interactive community of mutual support. Connecting this community is the Resident Expert Wall, which showcases individual student expertise and areas of strengths. At the Wall, students also list needs, questions, and struggles.

The Resident Expert Wall can be built throughout the year or for specific units of study and can be used for academic as well as social strengths and struggles. The choice is yours.

Here is how we get started:

♦ Give each student one, two, or three large index cards.

♦ Have students write their names and one strength on each card. Depending on grade level and whether you want them to share academic or social subjects, strengths could include anything from "multiplication facts" to "finding cool sites on the web" to "state capitals."

♦ Have them post these "Areas of Expertise" on the Wall.

♦ Give each student one to three additional index cards where they will list one need or question per card. Depending on grade level and topic, struggles could include anything from "getting started in writing" to "story problems" to "help organizing study materials."

♦ Students will return to the Wall often as their content needs and issues evolve.

Figure 2-1 The "Resident Expert Wall" is a wall or board in the classroom (perhaps a bulletin board) where students post their strengths and can seek help with their questions and needs. It shows students that everyone has something they can contribute to learning. When students know they can visit the Resident Expert Wall for resources and support, they discover how to collaborate and rely on someone other than the teacher.

Our Resident Experts

Nolan W. – Baseball trivia expert

Henry G. – Computer programming code-writer

Emma J. – Insect collector

Isaiah T. – Animal habitat expert

Amanda C. – Math problem-solver

Mackenzie S. – Cat care expert

Andrew B. – Camping/survival enthusiast

Jarett R. – Sci-fi/solar system expert

Belinda M. – Weather/storm tracker

Ameena N. – Spelling whiz

Robert N. – Extreme sports fan

Josh A. – Figure skater

Olivia C. – 50 state whiz

More Than Fluff

At this point, you might be thinking, "If this isn't strictly about a reading or writing workshop, then isn't this about centers? Is this about feel-good activities? Is this too fluffy? What are we supposed to teach?" To these we ask another question: Who is in charge of learning at your school? Who does the most work in your classroom? Who does the creating, constructing, producing, performing? The answer has to be—the learner. But is that really the case? Take a few minutes and explore the following:

♦ Do students manage themselves with little or no direction?

♦ Do students actively pursue their own questions?

♦ Do students problem-solve/troubleshoot?

♦ Do students prioritize independent tasks?

♦ Do students seek to understand?

If your answers were tentative, there is no need to place blame on students or yourself. "Learning" in the past is still heavily dependent on the teacher. Why is it that we equate our hard work as the teacher with rigor and true learning? The harder we work, the more we lecture and assign, the more our students will learn, right?

We should talk about experiences that students are mutually engaged in, involving lots of reading, writing, imagining, creating, calculating, constructing, producing, and performing—none of which are "fluff," and it is the student that is doing the most thinking. What if we unleashed this power and allowed students to take ownership of their learning? What if we let go of some control? If we want them to be responsible, interdependent and independent, than WE must let them "BE!"

♦ Be active

♦ Be strategic

♦ Be flexible

♦ Be mindful

♦ Be reflective

♦ Be purposeful

♦ Be courageous

- ◆ Be innovative

- ◆ Be engaged

- ◆ Be responsible and responsive

How do we reach a blend of letting students "BE" with enough assurances that students are learning what they must learn? We do it with a combination of skills, content, and passion.

4

A Passion-Driven Classroom: The Essentials

Expect the best, plan for the worst, and prepare to be surprised.

—Denis Waitley, Seeds of Greatness

When you walk into a Passion-Driven Clubhouse Classroom for the first time, it might take a few minutes to take in the scene. Before you are twenty or more students organized into small learning clubs as they explore a variety of projects that take the place of traditional learning centers and seatwork. Over on the side of the room in a space designated as the Math Lab, a group of children work together on dry-erase boards to solve a challenging math problem. They record their thinking on chart paper to share later.

On the other side of the room, something else is happening. In a cozy nook labeled, "Research Hub," a group of student-researchers gather around a laptop while making important notes in something called "thinking notebooks." As you step in a bit closer to observe the unfolding action, you find yourself intrigued as the children are debating the validity of a website's data: Is it a reputable source? Did we collect three resources to get a worthwhile answer? Have we used good-fit technology?

You hear students creating challenges and solving problems, employing the same thinking attitudes and behaviors of real-life mathematicians, scientists, and researchers. Novice scientists wrestle with the same issues that their real-life counterparts face when they encounter a new project or challenge. Not all work is in groups. You see individuals deeply engrossed in writing projects that are meaningful to them.

You also observe a focused area where passionate individuals are in a deep study. This space is labeled "The Passion Project." Most important, we see habits of both minds and hearts in action. The emphasis is placed on creativity, adaptability, perseverance, courage, and self-awareness. This is a far cry from the typical class participation grade for the teacher's grade book.

You will recognize that the center of conversation is drawn to the place where students regularly meet. It is clear that the thinking, sharing, and problem solving done collectively permeates their independent work.

You also take a moment to wonder, where was this place when I went to school? Where were the essential routines designed to represent and challenge a full spectrum of intelligences and interests? Yet, this is no haphazard implementation. In this classroom framework, with twenty or thirty students, the teacher must have specific learning goals centered on researched thinking strategies: inferring, determining importance, using schema, questioning, visualizing, monitoring understanding, and synthesizing information (Harvey & Goudvis, 2007; Keene & Zimmermann 1997).

You will hear questions and comments circulating throughout the day, such as

♦ Tell me about where you are in your work.

♦ What might happen if…?

♦ Can you picture a different way to do that? Tell me about it.

♦ What do you see as your group's challenge tomorrow?

♦ Can you find a new way to address the problem?

♦ What did you know that helped you accomplished that?

♦ How fantastic—you will need to record that and share!

Continuing along in your visit to the Clubhouse Classroom, you notice that across the room a small group of students you have been watching are called to a table tucked back in the corner. The teacher asks them to bring their work and begins to delve into the skills needed to improve their efficiency and efforts. Students are given clear direction, then leave ready to work smarter and with an increased confidence.

At a well-orchestrated transition time, the learners come together in a large group as apprentices as they engage in a lesson modeled by their Chief Learning Officer, the teacher. The C.L.O. connects the earlier work of the mathematicians with the math-content-area time, allowing the students to lead the discussion in the daily math problem solving. The members of the math club take center stage, sharing their notes, work, and thinking as the C.L.O. guides the discussion. Group reflection follows:

♦ So, let's hear an example.

♦ How would you suggest you go about this tomorrow?

♦ If you had advice for someone just beginning, what would it be?

- What did we discover was most important?

- What are we proud of?

The day continues with this flow of interdependent and independent learning opportunities guided by teacher coaching.

As you leave the classroom, you begin to think through what you observed. That initial excitement from the joy and laughter slows down, and you realize that sophistication and hard, rigorous learning occurred. You recollect the personal commitment it took to research and strategize, as well as the hard thinking involved in orchestrating this engaging learning environment.

Your visit ends with a small hand directing you toward the space where their special accomplishments and projects are displayed. You can't miss the calling of "Look what I did, let me show you this thing. Do you know what an oothica is?" and "Did you know that praying mantises eat their mates?" (See Figure 4-1 on page 40.)

At the teacher's direction, students reluctantly leave their projects for the day and come together again as a whole group. All will get to hear what was experienced, what was learned, and what challenges were met as well as what new gains and insights were discovered. After reflections are concluded, the teacher provides the class with time to collect their thoughts in the thinking notebooks. Tomorrow, it will all begin again.

As you can see, curiosity and inquiry drive the learning in the Clubhouse Classroom. The environment is organized specifically for more than an education, rather, an educational experience. This well-orchestrated framework ensures a combination of teacher-directed and student-directed learning through the following essentials that make it all work. Reflecting on the experience described, we see several essentials that must be in place to make it successful.

Essential #1: The Learning Clubs

Within the Passion-Driven Classroom, the small groups of individuals in Learning Clubs form a framework that enhances the clubhouse atmosphere, providing its members (our students) opportunities for learning-in-action. Learning Clubs are small heterogeneous groups of four to six students given a role for an extended period of time. In a self-contained, elementary classroom, we organize these small groups into content-area apprenticeships. For example, you might have a History Club for Social Studies work, a Math Club full of Mathematicians, and a Science Club full of Scientists. In a middle level or high school environment, the classroom periods are the Clubhouses, and

Figure 4-1   Thoughts about the Praying Mantis

> 9/13/07
> I think the praying mantis
> Either suck the Blad out of the grasshopper
> or maybe the grasshopper Just got Hungry
> because the gasshopper is dead. I notesed that
> the praying mantis is Always on top of the
> cage.
> —Abbie
>
>
> 9/24/2007
> I noticed both grasshoppers are dead.
> One has a hole in the thorax. I cannot
> find the beetles so I think they are
> dead.
> —Noah

the content area is sectioned into small, heterogeneous groups of Learning Clubs. For example, within the Language Arts Clubhouse Classroom, you will have a "Writers Club," and perhaps an "Editorial Club" for the school newsletter. Rather than going to English class, high school students are going to the "Journalism Club." The possibilities to fit together the content area, skills, and the kind of work and outcomes required are endless.

However, certain work is constant in all of the learning clubs, no matter the content area or grade level. All of the Learning Clubs are dedicated to helping students develop into better readers, writers, thinkers, collaborators, and, most important, passion-driven learners.

Students must develop patterns of thinking and develop habits in which their ability is combined with their inclination to think well and engage in metacognitive exercises. Students must have not only the opportunity to see passion-driven learning but also the experience of passion-driven learning and developing their own passions.

The Learning Clubs provide a context in which

♦ Thinking is valued.

♦ Time is reserved for thinking about our own and others' passions.

♦ Rich opportunities exist for exploring passion.

♦ Passion-driven learning is regularly modeled.

♦ The process as well as the products of thinking are present in the environment.

Just as important as the Learning Club itself are the tools of operations. The tools of The Learning Clubs support the type of work required of club members. What this work looks like depends on the grade level's essential skills and concepts, state standards, and again, are guided by student passion. They are also mirrored by the desired attributes and tools of their real-life counterparts. For example, you might see a Science Lab area where student-scientists practice answering a hypothesis by conducting observations and recording lab notes on a content-area science project. They are using the skills and competencies taught to them and that are used by practicing scientists. This hits practically any science standard in any curriculum, yet the science project may center on a specific student interest.

You might observe a Library area where student-journalists work to compose important details of the class or group-research questions about the mystery of the Bermuda Triangle. Students pour over maps and plot latitude and longitude on computer-generated simulations. These clubs change and rotate every two weeks so that students regularly practice the work of all the Learning Clubs.

Suggested club work areas of Learning Clubs include:

1. The Laboratory for the Scientists in the Science Club

2. The Library for the Journalists in the Writer's Club

3. The Research or Media Hub for Research from any of the Club Members

4. The Math Lab for the Mathematicians in the Math Club

5. The Archives for the Historians and Geographers working in the History Club and Geography Club

In addition, each Learning Club may visit more than one lab area or work space. The Researchers, for example, may need to visit the Archives area to locate needed information on what they are currently studying. Get the idea?

We are not prescribing the names and labels for the Learning Clubs, yet it is essential to have Learning Clubs where students work in teams practicing their passion and the craft of the content, whether they are elementary, middle, or high school students. Learning Clubs are essential to the Passion-Driven Classroom because they provide:

Interdependence. Students practice their learning passions collaboratively in teams.

Authenticity. Students read, write, speak, and listen for real purposes and real audiences and engage in cross-curricular thinking.

Digitally-Driven Learning. Student use technology as a tool.

Independence. Students have choice in how/what they study within the content.

Powerful learning experiences occur daily when we provide sufficient time and a classroom environment that lets kids "BE" learners.

Essential #2: The Opening Message and The Daily Boardroom Meeting

Just as teams in the adult workforce gather each morning with the C.E.O. of the company, students replicate real life and meet with their fellow learners and the Chief Learning Officer (C.L.O., aka teacher) to negotiate thinking and make decisions about learning. In the elementary classroom, this meeting happens in a designated corner or space of the room called the "Boardroom," where all the students can gather together as a whole group. At the middle level, one option is to have "Boards" of students, replacing the traditional "homeroom" practice.

Within this Boardroom meeting space, they work interdependently within the context of practicing the language and behaviors of a team. For example, students learn how body language affects discussion. Are arms folded in opposition or are they leaning in, listening respectfully to the individual making her case? Students practice the art of clarifying to seek understanding. Are they using phrases like, "I do not understand yet, can you please explain more?" or are they interrupting and telling their classmate how wrong they are in making their point? As a team member, are they taking responsibility to participate or are they refusing to speak or act? These are just a few examples of the essential life skills and collaborative behaviors they will practice and learn each day.

Students engage in the Opening Message daily routine, thinking about current issues in their community and the world around them. They learn how to speak to colleagues and work in a group as well as think critically about current issues. This daily Boardroom meeting is an upgraded Show-and-Tell. In a Learning Clubs Classroom, it is the Think-and-Tell time. For the older students, homeroom time is student and learning-driven, all focused on the Opening Message for the day's work.

Graves (1990) professes the power of inspiring our students to question and think about everyday events. It is these regular, daily happenings that spark our learners to write about topics for which they are passionate about.

The Opening Message routine focuses on:

A. What have you learned lately?

B. What tool did you use to get it?

C. What does this mean in the world?

The Boardroom meeting time and Opening Message are directed by the teacher's modeling of desired learning behaviors. Chapters 5 and 6 will provide explicit lessons that demonstrate how this is done. The C.L.O. provides a context to practice collaboration, makes plans for the day, then releases the learners to practice their passions in Learning Clubs, reconvening at the next Boardroom meeting to share what was learned. Most important, the C.L.O. reveals passion for learning and thinking about the world around us.

Essential #3: Reflection

Katie Charner-Laird, Sarah Fiarman, Frederick Won Park, and Sylvia Soderberg (2003), coauthors of the book *Cultivating Student Reflection*, describe reflection as "the mind's strongest glue" for making the connections essential to understanding, regardless of the subject matter:

> Reflection is the cornerstone of The Clubhouse Classroom. Stephanie Harvey and Anne Goudvis, coauthors of the book *Strategies that Work*, describe how students must be able to go beyond understanding a given learning strategy. They proclaim

that "they must know when, why and how to use it." (p. 16). Students reflect in the Clubhouse Classroom while practicing when, why and how to think in a variety of contexts.

Reflection activities may include any or all of the following (Later, we will describe the Thinking Notebook, which includes reflection as well.):

◆ Journaling

◆ Reflective papers

◆ Class discussions

◆ Small-group discussions

◆ Presentations

◆ Responses to course readings

◆ Responses to outside readings, media content, and experiences relevant to the issues surrounding the service activity

◆ Electronic discussions (e.g., chat, e-mail, online forum)

Varying activities will accommodate multiple learning styles and will help students understand reflection as part of the learning process, not as an isolated activity. Using a variety of tools, techniques, and even new media and technology offers us engaging ways to make reflection part of our content-area learning routines. From blogs to audio interviews—numerous ways exist and are developed each day that encourage and capture reflection.

Using technology to promote reflection has yet another benefit: A teacher can digitally archive student work, extending the reflection exercise beyond a single project or school year. (We love the idea of students coming back ten years from now and finding things they worked on—talk about the power of reflection!)

Regardless of methods or techniques, we have found the following questions effective to get students thinking and talking about the heart of learning:

◆ What did you learn and how do you know you learned it?

◆ What got in the way of your learning?

◆ What helped your learning?

◆ How did you feel? What are you going to do about it?

Essential #4: The Task Board

The task board displays the club membership (four to six students) in each Learning Club and a space for the individual club's weekly agenda. It is extremely simple. It can be as simple as a list on the dry-erase board, or a sentence-strip chart with manipulative cards.

The Club agendas can be inserted into clear plastic sleeves and displayed on a magnetic board next to the task board. These groups work together for approximately two weeks in order to delve deeper into their role before they change Clubs. This grouping process continues throughout the year.

Essential #5: Good-Fit Tools And Technology

We've heard of "good-fit books" (Boushy & Moser, 2006; Fountas & Pinnell, 1999). Students select books based on interest (their passion) and appropriate reading and thinking level. (We discuss strategies for using books later in this section.) The Learning Clubs Classroom has "good-fit technology" as well. Students learn how to use resources that are "the best fit" for pursuing their passions and for working within the Learning Club at the time.

Good-Fit Technology

When we started doing passion-driven work with students, resources were scarce. Now, the Internet is an amazing and fundamental resource for passion-driven teaching and learning, but can be overwhelming and time-consuming as busy schedules prevent us from having adequate time to find, organize, and investigate all there is available to us.

Wonderful and free resources available for nearly everything imaginable are waiting for you and your students! To get you started we have created an extensive but by no means all-inclusive list for you to begin exploring. See Figure 4-2 on the next few pages.

If you are new to integrating technology in your classroom, designing a project from scratch can be overwhelming, especially if the project is not about technology activities or lessons, but long-term student project work. You may want to browse sample projects, sample tasks, and lesson ideas to find an idea you can implement right away or even a project that fits with your curriculum.

Figure 4-2 Tools And Project Resources

Description: This list will get you started when matching your students to "good fit-technology."

Here are just a few examples of free resources and sites we visit on a regular basis. Most devoted to new web tools and discoveries– however you can easily find tutorial blogs and web sites on any subject imaginable by doing a simple Google search. Realize that many of these links are updated daily and may have been altered since we first included them in this book. It is always a good idea to view them before you allow students access. Start slow, preview, and enjoy the discovery!

We organized these valuable resources by Learning Club, however, several of them cross club borders and can be utilized in different ways:

Math Club Resources

Create graphs online http://nces.ed.gov/nceskids/createagraph/default.aspx

Interactive, math lesson creator http://enlvm.usu.edu/ma/nav/doc/intro.jsp

Two Programming sites www.alice.org and http://www.mathsnet.net/logo/turtlelogo/

Investopedia Stock Simulator http://simulator.investopedia.com

National Library of Virtual Manipulatives http://nlvm.usu.edu/

Financial Literacy at Kids Count: http://www.nfikidscount.org/

History Club Resources

www.ipl.org Internet Public Library

www.think.com Go look, and THINK! Create a collaborative learning project

www.mrdonn.org Includes a For Kids Section with links

Diary of the Planet http://www.earthweek.com/

The Smithsonian http://www.si.edu/museums/

Webquests and thinkquests http://thwt.org/webqueststhinkquests.html

Science Club Resources

http://www.amnh.org/ology/ The American Museum of Natural History: Astrology, paleontology, genetics

Figure 4-2 Tools And Project Resources (*continued*)

Science Club Resources *(con't)*

http://makezine.com A place to showcase inventions and all kinds of
 contraptions
Windows to the Universe http://www.windows2universe.org/
NASA www.nasa.gov/home/?flash=0
Weather and more: http://www.education.noaa.gov/sweather.html
Interactive physics simulations http://phet.colorado.edu/
Health: Kidnetic: http://www.kidnetic.com/

Geography Club Resources

Panoramic Views http://panoramas.dk/index.html check out the
 Grand Canyon!
National Geographic: Students will learn how to identify, compare,
 and appreciate the cultural characteristics of different regions
 and people. http://www.nationalgeographic.com/xpeditions/
 lessons/10/g35/tapestry.html
The Official Flat Stanley Project: Check out the Flat Stanley List of
 Participants to see where you can send a Flat Stanley or who might
 be sending a Flat Stanley to you. http://flatstanley.com/
KidAllies Follow our adventures as we travel around the Americas.
 Learn about different cultures and explore distant habitats. http://
 abren.org/kids/
Remove the classroom walls and go on an efield trip! http://www.
 efieldtrips.org/

Journalism Club Resources

Blue Zoo http://bluezoowriters.wordpress.com Geared to middle
 school and young teen writers. A place to publish work and for
 contests.
KidPub http://www.kidpub.com Billed as the largest collection of
 stories on the Internet; also offers an author forum.
Create your own printable magazine and ebooks: http://zinepal.com
Book talks online! Book trailers and movies for literacy http://www.
 homepages.dsu.edu/mgeary/booktrailers/default.htm

Figure 4-2 Tools And Project Resources (*concluded*)

Journalism Club Resources (*con't*)

Virtual Author Visits in Your Library or Classroom! http://
skypeanauthor.wetpaint.com/
www.visuwords.com (Visual Dictionary—Words are alive!)

Global Collaboration Resources:

Benjamin Franklin Institute of Global Education: The Mission of the
Franklin Institute is to accelerate, worldwide, innovative use of
technology in education and training so that the benefits of knowledge acquisition are affordable and accessible to all.

Global Teacher Project: Information and resources on global education

Project Based Learning on the Net: Bob Pearlman's project based
learning resources

Internet Projects: These curricular projects are designed and produced
by SchoolWorld members and our collaborative partners. All
projects are free of charge and are designed for use by international
schools. Read the project descriptions and subscribe to those that fit
the learning needs of your students!

ePals Classroom Exchange: ePALS is the Internet's largest community
of collaborative classrooms engaged in cross-cultural exchanges
http://www.epals.com

Just Good Stuff:

Here are a few links that were too great to leave out, but didn't fit a category:

says-it.com & makeagif.com (Make Seals & Animations)
googlelittrips.com (Use Google Earth with Literature)
www.mybrochuremaker.com (Brochure Maker)
www.wordle.net (Make Word Images)
draw.labs.autodesk.com/ADDraw/draw.html (Design!)
www.wikispaces.com & pbwiki.com (Make a Wiki)
edublogs.org (Blogs for School)
www.skype.com (Free Telephony via the Web)
k-12music.org (Tremendous Collection of Music)
etc.usf.edu/lit2go (Audio & PDF Literature)

Once you feel comfortable using technology tools in your classroom, you will be ready to jump into your own project design. We are fortunate to live in a time of information abundance. We have access to 24-hour news cycles and a preponderance of blogs and websites. We have plenty of things to share with students. Yet we also know that time is precious. We hope you will use the list of resources of our favorite resources as a starting point in your own journey.

Remember to Include Books!

Technology does not replace books, which remain a rich source of deep meaning. Both are powerful tools for learning.

How about you? How do you engage students in texts and tasks? What strategies work best for you and for your students? What about these?

- **Summarize:** Every once in awhile, you should stop, look at a portion of text you just read, and try to summarize the content in your own words. This is a good way to test your understanding of the material.

- **Make Predictions:** What do you predict will happen next? What will be the consequence? What do you base your predictions on? Is your prediction based on facts, feelings, experience, patterns you notice? Is a prediction different from a guess?

- **Formulate Opinions:** We have opinions on everything from the weather to politics. When you are reading, allow yourself to form opinions about the characters, the plot, the style of the writing. Share these opinions with others.

H.E.A.R.T.—A Strategy for Deep Meaning

With the end goal of comprehension, learners must be equipped with very specific skills and strategies. Using a technique we call HEART, we can ensure that students not only know those strategies but know when and where they need to be applied in the text or area of study. The elements of HEART can be taught singly or all together as students progress through more difficult texts.

We suggest that you start out by including all the elements of HEART so students see the active elements involved, and then later you might use the individual components to plan more differentiated strategy instruction. After several discussions and modeling sessions, the goal is for students to be able to access the elements of HEART internally and use them to remind themselves of meaningful reading, writing, and content study. These elements are the following:

H-Hold on! The first mistake students make happens in the first three seconds of reading expository text. They open the book, flip to the first page, and start reading word one. They proceed trying to gather facts, remember bold face words, and after a few short paragraphs, they find that there is no way to remember everything. They need to take a few seconds to "hold on." In fact, it is critical for students do the following three things **before** they read the first word!

1. Study the cover—what clues does it hint about the topic, author, and content?

2. Activate their schema—what do they already know about the these elements?

3. Consider the genre, text, and structure. A book on how to plant a seed is a very different reading experience than a book about photosythesis or the differences between tropical plants and exotic breeds. Students need to know that how the overall text or idea has been organized is significant. It influences the message and meaning and consequently their comprehension of it.

E-Eyes and Ears. To fully understand a text, you must view reading as an ACTIVE rather than a PASSIVE activity. In other words, just running your eyeballs over the words on a page does not mean you will comprehend the meaning of a text. We want readers to use their eyes and ears and notice the following:

♦ *Connections:* A good way to understand something that is new and unfamiliar to you is to connect it to something you already know or have experienced. Can you connect the text you are reading to a personal experience? Does it remind you of something else you've read or seen?

♦ *The Author's Craft:* As you are reading, you may notice certain things about the writer's style. Is there a lot of description? Is there too little description? Is the reading easy to follow or difficult in some way? Does the author use a lot of literary devices like similes and metaphors? Do you understand how and why the author is using such devices?

♦ *Patterns/Repetitions:* What do you notice about the way the text is structured? Do you notice some kind of pattern? Is there some element in the text that is repeated? What is important about this pattern or these repetitions? How does the structure contribute to the overall meaning?

A-Asking Questions. We do not want to set up the expectation that you are going to understand everything in the reading with complete clarity the first time through. Questions help us monitor and keep track of understanding as it is happening. What don't you understand? What confuses you? What words are unclear to you?

R-React/Reflect. Reading and learning are emotional commitments. Students can not see content as only facts and dates; rather they must constantly be thinking and wondering.

+ What do you notice?

+ What surprises you?

+ How do you feel about what you are reading?

+ What do you think about what you are reading?

T-Tell And Show. Do you find your students often learn a concept only to forget much of it a week after the test? To help your students develop concept mastery, it is important that they SHOW what they know and understand.

By following the HEART technique, you can see how the activity has meaning (a compelling why), how you could modify it by having small groups lead different strategies, and how you could improve the existing practice of reading nonfiction based on these strategic reading behaviors and actions.

New assessments of understanding are needed to measure 21st century skills and passion-driven learning objectives. We have found that the showing and telling, or performance, is the key. These performance-oriented tasks require students to reach beyond the literal meanings and interpretation by taking action on that meaning in artistic, creative, and critical ways.

The H.E.A.R.T. Technique

The following ideas in Figure 4-3 are active ways to show and tell what has been read and understood and models the HEART process with nonfiction study at the elementary and intermediate level.

Students demonstrate comprehension, that they have gotten to the HEART of text, when they can show evidence of the elements of heart (see Figure 4-3 on page 52).

Content is essential and is the compass that keeps learning focused. We can make our classroom environments learning powerhouses if we use the curriculum and standards as the foundation—and the students' passion—as

Figure 4-3 Getting to the Heart of Text: Content Area Standard
Assessment Rubric

Element	What Does This Really Mean?	How Will You Assess It?
H–Hold On! The student pauses and prepares for metacognitive work ahead.	Student will ♦ preview the text ♦ analyze the title ♦ attend to the author, illustrator, copyright information ♦ skim entire text or section for overall structure clues	Teacher Observation Learning Club journals Sticky notes with recorded and answers tabbed
E–Eyes and Ears The student prepares to actively engage with text, integrating clues from the language, structure, and their background knowledge.	Student will ♦ identify and use knowledge of common textual features (e.g., paragraphs, topic sentences, concluding sentences, glossary). ♦ identify and use knowledge of common organizational structures (e.g., chronological order, cause and effect). ♦ identify and use knowledge of common graphic features (e.g., charts, maps, diagrams, illustrations).	Student will ♦ highlight textual features and articulate their purpose. ♦ use graphic organizer to answer written/oral questions about the text. ♦ write a summary of the information presented in a graphic feature (constructed response).
A–Ask Questions The student makes insightful, clearly thought-out questions about the text, before, during, and after reading.	Student will ♦ ask various types of questions. ♦ use questions to help distinguish facts from opinion or fiction.	Student will ♦ use 2-column graphic organizer: What I read/What I wonder. ♦ record top three questions and share purpose in enhancing understanding. ♦ record what he or she is still wondering in Learning Club journal.

the driving force for learning. Honoring passion is more than simply giving students the technology, tools, and a few books on topics they find interesting. It is a commitment to helping students to discover for themselves—the emotional reasons linked to motivation that drive us to want to study or know something.

Figure 4-3 *(concluded)*

Element	What Does This Really Mean?	How Will You Assess It?
R–Read/React/Respond The student engages deeply with the text, interacting with the writer's voice, reacting and responding to the ideas while developing his or her own interests in the topic	Student will ♦ think and talk about the writer. ♦ use the writer's name. ♦ use conversational words like, "really, interesting, I never though of it that way, I see how…" as though in a conversation with the author. ♦ Student is involved cognitively and emotionally.	Conferencing peer and teacher Rubric (informal assessment) Students provide the commentary along with the information about the topic—sharing their thoughts and opinions in small group or in writing
T–Tell and Show	Assesses understanding beyond literal measures of true false and fill in the blank. We are looking for students' synthesis of ideas and interpretations of the topics.	Conferencing peer Performance Task Group or individual Project Formal presentation—written or oral

Essential #6: Celebration

Celebrating hard work and perseverance is an important part of any learning, and it is not taken lightly in the Passion-Driven Classroom. We try to move beyond the traditional "Good job's" and "Way-to go's" while still ensuring that immediate and positive feedback happens often. Celebrations are more than a confirmation of learning completed; they lift the spirits of both you and your students and create excitement about the next learning adventure. Below are some of our favorite "passion-inspired" celebrations you can do with your students.

Model these first yourself, and then give students a chance to try them out on one another:

♦ **The Silent Cheer.** Wave arms around excitedly and "shout" with no sound coming out of your mouth.

♦ **The Hearty Handshake.** In pairs, students do a 30-second hearty handshake, shaking hands wildly.

♦ **The Magic Touch.** In pairs, students touch index fingers together while saying "YYYeeessss!"

- ♦ **"I Appreciate You Because. . . ."** Write each of your students a note of appreciation, acknowledging a particular effort or achievement.

- ♦ **The Exclamation.** Say encouraging words like "Faaaan-tas-tic!!!"

- ♦ **The Arnold.** In perfect Schwarzenegger stance—biceps flexed, chests out, arms forward—yell out a big "Yeah! We'll be back!!"

- ♦ **A "Round" of Applause.** Move your arms around in a large circular motion while clapping your hands. Next you can try a "square," "triangle," or "rectangle" of applause.

Many of the previous tips have been adapted from workshops we have attended and from research on how the brain learns. We have found creating your own is even more motivating and fun. So tap into your creative side and let your students give it a go. The end result is not only novel but will enhance learning and memory of all they worked hard to achieve.

Doing and Being

Pulling all of this information together, we realize that learning success is really about "DOing AND BEing": Success in the Passion-Driven Classroom is not simply a matter of choosing what to know, but requires learners to make choices on how and who to "be." Our daily lives are filled with choices, but "BE" choices are different that "DO" choices. For example, we can choose to watch TV, read a book, finish an assignment. These are observable, concrete, and are often obvious to an outside observer. "BE" choices are more subtle and not easily described or discussed; therefore, we spend less time thinking about them and consequently are less prepared to make them purposefully and successfully.

Let's explore these choices both in and out of school. We can make a choice to visit an old friend; one we have not seen for some time. That is a DO choice. We are doing it, making the arrangements, getting in our cars, and committing to the experience. Here's the "BE" choices involved: We can BE excited, showing our friend how happy we are to see them after all this time. We can BE curious, asking lots of questions about their life, family, and work. We can also BE jealous, acting aloof and envious of our friend's successful accomplishments. We can BE rude, rolling our eyes, letting out a sigh or too, even trying to act as if we really don't care as our friend shares all the new and wonderful things that happened since we last spoke. We can BE deceitful, making exaggerations of our life experiences or painting a little too-perfect picture of how things are going when in truth they are not so rosy.

As adults, we make "do" and "be" choices all the time with varying levels of awareness and control. It is important that we make the difference public for students, such as giving personal and academically related examples of "DO" and "BE" choices like the following.

Teacher   Students, let's say you had an upcoming assignment. It was a content area project you had been working on for some time. The assignment weighed heavily on your grade.

Your "DO" choices have been clearly laid out for you:

You will do the research.

- ♦ You will find six sources.
- ♦ You will have both visual and textual examples backing up your findings.
- ♦ You will... (you get the idea)

Your grade will be determined MORE by your "BE" choices:

- ♦ Will you be curious?
- ♦ Will you be creative?
- ♦ Will you be daring?
- ♦ Will you be willing to ask for help, take a different direction, alter the strategies you are using?
- ♦ Will you be excited about the things that go wrong, because you know that you will learn from them?
- ♦ Will you be diligent and demanding of yourself, committing 110% to the work?

Helping students understand and choose to "be" will affect not only their achievement but overall content area and learning experiences as well. Students are going to need our help, so both their "DO" and "BE" decisions can be conscious, purposeful, and productive.

We suggest the following:

1. Create a "TO BE" Chart with words like:

   - ♦ Energetic
   - ♦ Excited
   - ♦ Interested

- Curious

- Relaxed

- Calm

- Confident

- Thoughtful

- Creative

- Innovative

- Helpful

Students can generate definitions depicting how this looks, sounds, and feels including photos and images that bring the "BE" decisions to life

2. Role Play. Each week during reflection time students could bring an experience to the group and discuss "choices of doing and being." Remember that choosing a way to BE increases the chances of actually being that way. The following frames can help scaffold that discussion:

- I need to do _____. I could chose to be _____
  or _____.

- Here is the difference in the outcome _____.

OR put another way:

- By choosing to BE _____, here is what happened while
  I was doing _____.

Either way, we want students to know that choices have consequences. Each of us has a choice to make in how we want to be. We have the opportunity to change our choices as much or as little as we want. Choosing how to be. And being a passionate learner is a CHOICE!

So the next time you hear students say, "Teacher, teacher, what do we need to do?" and "How are we going to do it?," your response might be "That depends, students, what are you willing to BE? What tools will you use? Remember, that choice is yours!"

5

Organizing the Clubhouse Classroom

Organizing is what you do before you do something, so that when you do it, it is not all mixed up.

—A.A. Milne (author Winnie-the-Pooh series)

In the Clubhouse Classroom, everything has a purpose, organizational detail is key, and member input in critical. With this in mind, we strive to integrate the arrangement of physical space, purposeful tools, and meaningful routine. Our desire is to create an environment that feels like a close community and allows student inquiry to thrive. Our ultimate goal is to provide an environment in which students are allowed and able to practice their passions—the clubhouse atmosphere of Learning Clubs described earlier.

The Physical Environment

The Boardroom Meeting and Learning Club Spaces

Our classrooms come in many shapes and sizes. No matter how big or small the space, the physical layout is key to the success of the passion-driven, clubhouse classroom. We love to incorporate interesting furniture, tables, and light in our classrooms. Even though we may have the physical environment all planned and everything in its place on day one, the students (the club members) show up with their own ideas and so we make changes. The following ideas are meant as a guide to begin designing the work space.

We plan the physical arrangement for the Boardroom meeting and the Learning Club spaces together since each affects how much room is dedicated to the other. Will a large carpet space be set aside for the Boardroom meetings? How will you convene your Boardroom meeting each day? Since teacher modeling and shared thinking are critical to the Boardroom meeting tasks, there needs to be enough space for everyone to sit in a circle or arrange the desks in a circle. Everyone should be able to see the C.L.O. and the learning tools demonstrated. What learning tools will you use during the Boardroom meetings? Many anchor charts are developed in the beginning Boardroom meeting lessons. A large chart tablet is included in the meeting space. As C.L.O., the teacher is seated or stands in a central location where all can see and hear the modeled thinking as well as see the modeled writing.

The center of the classroom can be left open with the desks arranged around this space. Another arrangement is to leave a corner in the classroom for these meetings that has a dry-erase board. At the middle or high school level, the Boardroom meeting may take the place of teaming time in homerooms or can serve as the opening to the content area block of time. Students can arrange desks quickly into an oval or circle and can move them back when the meeting concludes.

Once the Boardroom meeting space is set aside, then plans for the Learning Club work areas are developed. How many Clubs will you create and utilize? This depends on your grade level and content standards/curriculum. We have used five Learning Clubs in our classroom and labeled the work areas the following: The Archives for the Historians, The Science Lab for the Scientists, The Library for the Journalists, The Math Lab for the Mathematicians, and the Archives for the Geographers. In classrooms with limited space, the Learning Clubs materials can be dispersed throughout the classroom on small tables or in portable tubs. Students in this set-up begin at the Learning Club, yet can move to a different place in the room to conduct their work.

Learning Club	The Club Work Area	The Apprentices
The Math Club	The Math Lab	The Mathematicians
The Writers Club	The Library	The Journalists
The History Club	The Archives	The Historians
The Geography Club	The Archives	The Geographers
The Science Club	The Science Lab	The Scientists

The Task Board Area is where the student names are displayed in the Learning Clubs as well as an area for the clubs to publish their weekly agenda. Sentence strip holders work well with index cards. Another option is to use magnetic tape and names on the side of a file cabinet. The Task Board area, if possible, should be located close to the Opening Message so that the students' eyes move logically from the first part of the day to the next.

The Inspiration Station

Only a few students each day formally share their thinking and new learning in the daily Boardroom meeting. The Inspiration Station is a place where, throughout the day, any students can post their thinking and inspirations. There are times in the day when some students complete tasks faster than others. Rather than pulling out another worksheet, students may visit this station. The station also serves as a place from which to gather information and inspiration for their thinking notebooks. Post a large sheet of bulletin board paper below the dry-erase board in your classroom or on the back of the door, for example.

The lesson to explain how this is used with students sounds like the following:

Teacher This is your Inspiration Station, a place to bank your inspiration. You know that the kind of bank we usually talk about is a place to store your money for later use. This is the place to store your thoughts and inspirations for your later use. What happens when you didn't get to share your learning at the Boardroom meeting but you just can't wait to share? You could record it in your thinking notebook, but you could also put it here. This is a public place to write it. What happens when you are working in your Learning Clubs and you think you found something another Club might need? Putting it in your thinking notebook wouldn't make sense. You can post it here instead. You will add ideas from this station to your thinking notebook as well.

The teacher may choose not to grade or critique this work. It will be used for idea seeking purposes; however, it can also be part of a weekly homework assignment to be checked for completion.

Here are some possibilities for Inspiration Station:

♦ Family stories or traditions

♦ Interesting things you have seen or heard

♦ Close observations of people, objects, sights, sounds, moods, tastes

♦ Memories

- Experiences with friends, family, classmates

- Celebrations or victories

- Dreams

- What fascinates you

- Fantasy/things that you imagine, wish for

- Things you are proud of

- Things that are easy and things that are hard

- Things you are an expert in and things you would like to know more about

- The first time you ever did something and the last time you ever did something

- Things you do all the time and things you don't do all that often

As the Inspiration Station fills up, you can take a digital photo and print it in an Inspiration Station notebook and place it in the Archives.

Grouping Students in Learning Clubs

For the very first Learning Club combinations, the teacher will group students using the information from Phase One of Launching the Learning: Passion Discovery (Chapter 6 will explain how to conduct these lessons.) The information is synthesized from the individual Talent Portraits, rankings of workstations, and other informal observations to fit the students into either their first or second choices for the first round of Learning Club work. Students will stay in this Club, ideally, for two weeks. Clubs then change. Each group moves to a different club for the next two weeks. It is important to stick to this two-week rotation so that all students experience multiple Learning Club roles and practice the work of apprentice mathematicians, journalists, and so on.

The Students' Seating/Desk Arrangement

We highly encourage you to use the Learning Clubs to dictate where students sit. Remember, a Learning Club consists of four to six students for an extended period of time. As we stated earlier, if we want our students to be responsible, interdependent and independent, than WE must let them "BE!" Rather than separating them, we keep them together to work through their issues, problems, and challenges. Allowing students to sit as a Learning Club also minimizes time lost in transitions moving from desk to small group to large group and back again.

Clubhouse Tools

It may take a while for your students to get into the practices and routines of the Clubhouse Classroom. They are used to sharing discoveries with their close friends before school, after school, at recess, on the computer and phone at night, but not necessarily with their teacher and peers at school during the actual school day. The following tools are supplements to add to the environment and enrich the learning experience.

Key Reflection Tool: The Student Thinkbook

Traditionally, we ask children to keep records of their "schoolwork" in binders, planners, and notebooks where they record assignments, material, due dates, tests, and quizzes, but when do they keep a record of how they learn? Who are they becoming as learners? Where do they track their discoveries, passions, and talents?

Lewis and Clark, Christopher Columbus, Da Vinci, and Einstein carried many valuable instruments with them as they made discoveries and shared them with the world. Their singlular most important tool was their notebook. Lewis and Clark titled theirs "The Journey of Discovery." We have the opportunity to do the same, and in this amazing journey, we hope that their thinking notebooks will help them discover new worlds, chart new territory, and lead them to treasures around and within themselves.

Inspired by these great minds, we have designed the Student Thinkbook to teach learners to take responsibility for their individual thinking and learning in an authentic way, to prompt inquiry, and to inform instruction. Recording moments of individual and collective genius serves as a window into students' minds as they navigate through Learning Clubs, and this process is likely to become a lifelong habit and skill.

Each student has a large, bound notebook, a spiral notebook, or a heavy-duty, three-pronged folder used strategically throughout the day. Even if your school uses laptops for learning, or has a one-to-one laptop ratio, it is still important to have a tangible, written tool. This is the place where learners keep ongoing lists, sketches and doodles of their interests and passions, websites, workstation logs, and other tools. The notebook can be made ahead of time or tabbed by the students with specific sections marked as they go.

Although there is no prescription for the section labels, it is essential that the tabbed sections mirror the content areas taught and the Learning Clubs in the classroom. We suggest the following Thinkbook components. Lessons for each of these components will be described in detail in the next chapter.

Following is an example of the sections of a Thinkbook.

My Thinkbook

Thomas

Front Cover: Photographs of the students in their "thinking poses." (The teacher photographs each student posed in his or her best thinking facial expression.)

Inside Cover: Club Rules—a copy of the Boardroom Bylaws and Classroom Manifesto developed by the class.

First Page: Letter from the teacher about thinking and pursuing your passion

Section 1: My Passion Profile

    A. Talent Profile Interview

    B. Passion Lists: Things I know about and things I want to learn about

    C. Heart Map

Section 2: The Learning Clubs (Each section will reflect what the teacher has developed as learning club titles. Remember, it matches the content and curriculum.)

    A. Mathematician Section

        1. 3 Biography Passion Profiles

        2. Math Glossary

        3. Math Tools Record

    B. Historian Section

        1. Timeline templates (to record ongoing historical events studied at the workstations and during content work time)

        2. 3 Biography Passion Profiles

        3. History Tools Record

    C. Scientist Section

        1. 3 Biography Passion Profiles

        2. Science Tools Record

    D. Geographer Section

        1. State Map

        2. World Map

        3. Continents

        4. Geography Tools Record

    E. Journalist Section

        1. Cool & Amazing Quotes List

        2. Beautiful Language section

        3. Journalism Tools Record

Section 3: Lots of blank paper to use as needed, for example, a student may create a timeline, a Venn diagram to compare and contrast an area of study, or jot down thoughts to save later.

Note that each of these Learning Clubs notebook sections has a Tools Record, a place to record websites, books, magazines, TV shows (episodes), noteworthy iTunes, safe blogs of interest, and other specific resource tools.

Consider the Student Thinkbook as the new and improved tool that replaces the mundane worksheet that we traditionally mandate in our classrooms. The Thinkbook is used within the context, and at the moment, of learning. Adapt it for your grade level, school, and own teaching style. This is the most important guide to instruction and student learning, and the students are the authors. It contains ideas they find and record because these ideas are important to them. Their selections accumulate into a body of knowledge that informs instruction and gives the students real power in their fields of interest.

Figure 5-2 Club Members Write to their Teacher.

Dear Mrs. S.

I think they would look like these.
1. It will get bigger.
2. It will get taller.
3. A leaf will come out

sincerely,
Riley

Dear Mrs. Sandvold.

I think the seed coat will come off and the leaves will sprout down a little. I also think in a little bit a flower will sprout and a little after that that beans. peas. and corn will come out.

Sincerely.
Courtney

The Club Thinkbook

Each of the Learning Clubs also has a Club Thinkbook that stays in the club work area. These document daily learning and thinking done in student groups as they work in the Learning Clubs each week. In these books, there is a section where the club members write to the teacher about their learning in that specific club. (*See* Figure 5-2)

Another more formal record keeping sheet can also be utilized. Modeled after scientific inquiry, we have designed the record keeping and reflection sheet in Figure 5-3 on page 66.

Each Club Thinkbook includes a running list of tools as well as graphic organizers at the Learning Club work area so that they can employ these as they work and write in the Club Thinkbook. For example, the Historians may need to keep a timeline of events as they study an important time in history. Blank timelines are available as a tool, as well as digital timeline resources. We suggest using a large binder for each of the Club Thinkbooks.

Since the students change Learning Clubs every two weeks, this tool allows for ongoing record keeping and synthesizing work over time. Club Thinkbooks are left behind at the end of each school year and become the archives and club research record for the new group. You can make this as detailed or simple as desired, depending on the grade level, subject, and purpose. We use a simple approach so that time is spent more on the thinking and collaboration in the clubs. The procedure for using the Club Thinkbook is the following:

1. At the beginning of every Club time, a member of the Club reads what was recorded the day before about their topic.

2. Next, they read aloud the Club's questions, discoveries, and answers.

3. Then, they decide what they are going to do based on the group agenda that they set at the beginning of the week in the Boardroom meeting.

4. They work on the agreed upon tasks.

5. At the Closing part of the day, the Club reconvenes and adds anything to the Club Thinkbook record.

The Clubhouse Classroom Routine Sequence

Routines need to be taught explicitly, step by step (a little secret no one told us when we first started teaching!) Finding the balance between passionate pursuits and mandated curriculum is no easy task either. Students need

Figure 5.3 Learning Club Agenda

	Our Agenda We are studying:	**Our Questions, Discoveries, and Answers:**
Week of: _____ Club Members: Members Absent: Date Name	Our Tasks this Week: • • • • • • • • •	
Learning Tools Learning tools we've used:	**HELP!** We need help:	**Tips for the Next Club**

a predictable structure and a routine in order to learn so they can become more independent. When a class has a predictable structure and can manage routines with confidence, the class has more flexibility to accommodate spontaneous and passionate endeavors.

We have highlighted each of the following components earlier in our descriptions of the Clubhouse Classroom. Now we put these together in a suggested sequence. With a little patience and the following daily routine, your class will be well on its way.

1. The Opening Message: Learning Now!

Passion doesn't have to be manufactured: Passion emerges naturally from the practice of learning in its natural state and context, and we accomplish this in the daily opening message.

Think about what we usually do with the first 15 to 20 minutes of class each day: attendance, calendar, lunch count, and so on. Not very passionate, is it? How can we use this time instead to stimulate imaginations, release mental energy, and stay motivated and excited for the entire 180 days? Is that even possible?

Rather, using the idea of Learning Now!, students are instructed to search for new or interesting information and have it ready for the Boardroom meeting. They write on a chart in different colored markers as they come into the classroom, type it, and project the list, or record it in their Thinkbook. The following list was generated by fourth graders at the end of a school year.

My mom and I put up my batting cage wrong. We did it backwards.

There was an accident on highway 20 last night at 10 p.m.

A Robin's egg is blue.

A Slice of Pizza at the store is $1.69 and so are potato wedges.

There are lots of movies based on the year 2012. People are dissing that year for some reason.

TCU is going to the College World Series for the very first time!

That instead of having 8 people in one hotel room, there is four rooms and two people in each room at a basketball camp I'm going to go to this summer.

My Dad is taking me out to dinner of my choice for helping him.

There is 47 grams of sugar in my favorite candy.

I know how to make an igoogle page!

I found out we're going to Florida next year.

Homeless kids live in cars sometimes.

In 1889 a gold nugget was found in Montana.

Montana has the Roe River. It's the shortest river in the world.

The Arkansas/Texas state line goes through the town of Texarkana.

Let us demonstrate the way we start every day in the Passion-Driven Classroom. In the last 24 hours we have learned that:

"Tonight, if my favorite baseball team wins, they will go to the World Series! The odds are pretty great they can win it because..."

"Did you know that if you put your jack-o-lantern outside, bugs live in it? I wonder if the candle I put inside of it will hurt them?"

"I learned that metal is edible in Ripley's Believe it or not. I wonder how this can be true?"

"I didn't realize what the Boston Tea Party really was! I wonder if this type of thing could ever happen again."

What the Opening Message clearly illustrates is how much there is to know from our past, and how much the world is changing right now and will continue to change, and the world will change a whole lot more by the time you finish this chapter. This simple and fast paced opening routine guarantees passion will emerge with something that will engage the body, mind, and heart, and it will be centered on important content, skills, and knowledge! Accordingly, the work in the Opening Message is all about this critical and passionate current learning. Let us take you deeper:

When students walk in the classroom, a question is displayed. Today's posted question asks: What have you learned since yesterday? Students write, sketch, or draw and label a diagram in their thinking notebooks or even blog about their recent learning. We spend the next few minutes sharing what we have learned, discovered, read, seen, heard, and viewed in the last 24 hours of our learning lives.

Why do we start the day with this routine? Learning is not an endeavor just for school. It is learning that fuels our lives. It brings the outside to the inside of the classroom and vice versa. Learning is perpetual, continuous, and requires us to be active contributors. The daily Opening Message does more than allow students a context to share tidbits of cool information. It's all about the inquiry and conversation. Students get so excited about what they are learning right now, they want to share it with the world.

The daily Opening Message and the Learning Now! routine is:

- grounded in the lives of our students
- critical and relevant
- participatory and action oriented
- experiential and inviting
- enticing and curious
- challenging
- hopeful and joyful
- visionary
- academically rigorous
- igniting critical inquiry

The morning sharing inevitably leads to follow-up questions like

- How/Where did you find that?
- Who told you?
- How do you know this to be true?
- Could we do that?
- What do we need?
- What if?

All of this leads us into demonstrations of how we sift, sort, prioritize, and take action on knowledge while simultaneously showcasing the extraordinary power of learning tools and technology. This new start to the day not only lights a spark of excitement and energy, it sets the tone, the expectation, and it extends the invitation to "Join the Learning Club," which is how we frame the rest of the day as we spend our time together figuring out how to make sense of this amazing world and the people who inhabit it.

2. The Daily Boardroom Meeting

The daily Boardroom meeting allows the teacher a context in which to gradually release responsibility and supports the students in their Clubhouse

Learning. Discussion and verbalizing metacognition are at the center of this procedure. Discussions serve as anchor experiences to assist students with their daily tasks. "The art of discussion is noted as one of the most neglected language arts in school" (Meyer, 2006). Learning Now! discoveries are shared, discussed, and Learning Club tasks are set up and debriefed. It is where shared thinking and learning occurs.

3. The Learning Clubs

After the daily Boardroom meeting, students know where to go and with whom they are working. They have a general idea what they will do once they are convened in the specified Learning Club area (for elementary) or Content Clubhouse Classroom (middle and high school).

4. Content Connections

We refer to *content time* in the elementary classroom as the traditional chunks during the day in which the content area instruction occurs, and to *content classes* at the middle and high school levels. Think of reading, writing, and arithmetic with science and social studies worked in. Remember that the content expectations/curriculum are the foundation for learning and student passion drives the learning.

If you are used to having a reading and/or writing workshop, you would schedule content connection time at the content area time. For instance, during the workshop, students would be independently reading and working either together or alone at a Learning Club as they wait for their small group reading time. Their tasks may be specific to something modeled in the reading workshop. Perhaps the teacher is delving into a unit of study during Language Arts on "determining importance in nonfiction." Students gather in the Learning Clubs to practice "determining importance" as a historian, mathematician, or researcher. Content connections take place during the explicit time of the day when math is taught. The teacher might have designated days or times when individuals or groups that need differentiation visit the Math Club.

Consider this other variation. Instead of a study hall at the middle and high school levels, a block of time is designated for a specific club time. The key is that during the content area time, we are thinking, acting, and using the language of Mathematicians, Scientists, Writers, and so forth during explicit content times, so that passionate learning is seamless throughout the day. Everything is connected by this mindset.

5. The Closing

Just as we maximized time at the beginning of the day, we end the day in the Clubhouse Classroom with a bang, making every minute count. In Passion-Driven Classrooms, students beg to learn and work more. They want more time to practice their passion. The closing in the passion-driven classroom is focused on extending learning into the next day and beyond. Students are reminded of "Learning Now!" and are charged with having something new, cool and interesting to share the next day. Sometimes they are revisiting a Boardroom or club task and making notes for the next day.

As you can see, every section of the day has purpose and is driven by meaningful, passion-driven work that is grounded in the content and standards. Passionate learning goes beyond roles and routines. For passion to survive it needs structure. But for structure to grow, it needs passion. The daily routine is extremely critical to the success of The Passion Driven Classroom and deserves attention.

Passion From Day One:
Simple Changes = Big Impacts

Passion-driven learning can take place only in certain settings and in an environment where the passionate beliefs and actions of all learners are valued and recognized. Small, purposeful actions can make a significant difference. Chapter 6 will move you through three phases of instruction to explicitly teach and launch the Clubhouse Classroom. The remainder of this chapter includes lessons that you can use tomorrow to begin transforming your classroom in passionate ways with simple tweaking in the way we do things.

Consider this:

♦ Does your classroom invite students to come in to look around and say, "Hey, look AT THIS!" "WOW- This is AWESOME!!!" or "WHEN do we get to…"

♦ How do the students perceive your classroom? Are there indications of your own passions—and potential to share theirs?

♦ When students enter your school or classroom, what are the first things they see? Are there celebrations of their achievements, samples of their projects, evidence of their value and involvement?

Invite Students to Create the Classroom Environment

This approach to setting up the environment is not appropriate for all grade levels or teachers. Read the following as an example of a continuum of how you might invite student input into the classroom environment.

As students enter the classroom on the first day, the walls are bare, the tables and chairs are placed along the sides of the room, the books and materials are still enclosed in crates and boxes. There are shelves, cabinets, racks, and organizers waiting for their perfect place.

As students walk in, somewhat surprised by our "under preparation," we invite them to join us at the shared meeting space we have intentionally positioned at the center of the room. We pull up our teacher chair and invite them to the first of what will be many learning club meetings. We explain that we, students and teacher, will be the architects and designers of our learning experience, beginning with how and where we will be doing our work.

We make a list of the key "areas," the critical supplies, and the necessary elements each will require. Students break up into small groups, assign a project manager, and begin to craft the conditions that will allow them to engage with one another, the content, and materials.

The Crucial Conversation

For the first few days, the creation of our physical space begins to emerge, leading us into conversations about the routine, roles, and responsibilities needed to keep our community fully engaged and functioning. As we gather for our daily meeting, midway in the week, the students' attention is drawn to a large, colorful sign that reads:

PASSIONATE LEARNING HAPPENS HERE

We ask students what they think this sign is saying and we talk about the words and how they might affect our time together. We let the sign be for a few days as we ponder how passion influences the way we work, what we study, how we study, and how we grow together individually and as a classroom.

This conversation serves as the foundation for what will become our Learning Club Bylaws—a declaration of what we value and intend to accomplish this coming year. As the weeks progress we collect and formalize the thoughts and ideas as they emerge from our conversations.

To create the sign, we write the words " PASSIONATE LEARNING HAPPENS HERE" along the top of a large piece of butcher paper divided into the following columns:

Individually	Our Classroom	Our School	Our World

We add our ideas and perspectives over the course of the next several weeks until we have formalized how passion influences and binds together these worlds. It is an important discussion and well worth the time and effort as it will critically affect the way we operate and engage the rest of the year.

We have found the following books to be powerful additions to the conversation:

♦ *The Giving Tree*, Shel Silverstein
♦ *Hey World, Here I Am*, Jean Little
♦ *Ish* , Peter Reynolds
♦ *The North Star*, Peter Reynolds
♦ *If I Were in Charge of the World*, Judith Voirst
♦ *I'm in Charge of Celebrations*, Byrd Baylor
♦ *Swimmy*, Leo Leoini
♦ *The Important Book*, Margaret Wise Brown
♦ *Only One You*, Linda Kranz
♦ *Another Important Book*, Margaret Wise Brown
♦ *You Are Important*, Todd Snow
♦ *The Wonder of You*, Nancy Tillman
♦ *Always*, Ann Stott
♦ *The Three Questions*, Jon Muth
♦ *Courage*, Bernard Waber
♦ *What Do You Do with a Tail Like This?*, Robin Page
♦ *Hey you! C'mere! A Poetry Slam*, Elizabeth Swados
♦ *I Like Myself*, Karen Beaumont
♦ *People*, Peter Spier
♦ *We the Kids Preamble to the Constitution*, David Cattrow
♦ *Hey World Here I Am*!, Jean Little
♦ *Every Living Thing*, Cynthia Rylant
♦ *Journey*, Patricia MacLachlan

As the year progresses and our community evolves, we will refer back to these first days often and remember, through the ups and downs, that all students will know that passion matters and that we teachers take both their minds and hearts seriously.

Rules or Manifesto?

A manifesto is a document written by a group or individual that publicly declares their goals, rules, and guidelines for life. Random House defines manifesto in this way: "a public declaration of intentions, objectives, or motives."

Words are the ambassadors of our intentions. Crafting the manifesto is more than a crafty way to come up with classroom rules. It is in the process of making public what we value, believe, and hope for that we define our behaviors and actions. Creating our class manifesto is a commitment to the actions that move us closer to our individual and community goals, and it will keep us focused on the goals that matter most and remind us of where we are going. Here is an example of how you might introduce the concept of a manifesto.

Student Assignment: Writing A Personal Manifesto—Self Portrait of a Passionate Learner

Teacher   Your manifesto is your own roadmap to a better learning future. You write the rules, you set the bar, and you determine your goal and dreams. It is usually one page or less, with bullet points, straight to the point, and covering all aspects of your life and learning you want to improve on and grow.

Consider your manifesto to be a set of rules or commandments which you will follow in order to accomplish your personal best. Having a personal manifesto will help you make decisions that are in line with your values and the vision you have for your learning and life. Your manifesto should be a document you can read many times. It should also be flexible so that you can update it as your life develops.

Your manifesto should be posted somewhere in your room and should be openly shared with others who are curious.

Based on what you learn about yourself as a learner and about yourself in our community of learning, consider the following elements for your Manifesto:

- What are your important life questions?
- What are your goals?
- What is most important for you to know or do better this year?
- How you will pursue the answers to these questions?
- What will you stand for in your pursuit of these goals?
- What won't you stand for in your pursuit of these goals?

Make your manifesto clear and powerful. Be creative, honest, open, and inspiring! Remember, this is YOUR Manifesto. You will know you have succeeded when you are personally touched, moved, and inspired by your own words. You are writing this for YOU, not for a grade!"

Here are examples of Student Learning Manifestos:

My Learning Manifesto: _Jordon_
1. Think Big
2. Practice Hard
3. Stay Positive
4. Don't Dwell on Mistakes Long
5. Share What You Know
6. Collaborate

My Learning Manifesto: _Conner_
1. Ask a Great Question everyday
2. Read Tons!
3. Writer Tons!
4. Be a Good Listener
5. Try Something New and Hard at least once a week
6. Practice Tons!

My Learning Manifesto: _Sol_

1. Write Down All My Ideas
2. Write Everyday
3. Read Everyday
4. Keep Organized
5. Give Myself a Compliment

Heart Maps

Passionate learners do not always wear their passion on their sleeves, but keeping our hearts open is necessary for our work. When we write about, speak about, and read things we care deeply about, we are more successful.

We love the idea of Heartmapping from the amazing Georgia Heard (1999, p. 108–109) as a way to make this visible to students. Creating a heart map is a way to help students visualize and make concrete what they really care about and wish to pursue as well as an important practice for bringing us closer as a community.

Listen in as Georgia describes the power of the process to young poets:

> Yesterday, we spoke of how poets write from their hearts. Today, I was thinking about how sometimes poets have to do some work first to know what's in their heart, to know what they really care about, and what's really important to them. So, we are going to do something very different—we are going to make a map of our hearts.
>
> Today I'd like you to make a map of all the important things that are in your heart; all the things that matter to you. You can put people and places you care about; moments and memories that have stayed with you; things you love to do; anything that has stayed in your heart because you care a lot about it.

She suggests using the following questions to help get students started:

♦ What really affected your heart?

♦ What people have been important to you?

♦ What are some experiences or central events that you will never forget?

♦ What happy or sad memories do you have?

- What secrets have you kept in your heart?

- What small or big things are important to you? (Heard, 1999)

As students display and share who they are and what they are most passionate about, Heard (1999) suggests that they explore these additional questions:

- Should some things be outside the heart and others inside?

- Do you want to draw more than one heart? Happy or sad? Secret or open?

- What's at the center of your heart? What occupies the outer edges?

- Do different colors represent different emotions, events, or relationships?

- Are there parts of your heart you are willing to share with others? Parts you want to keep private? How will you represent both?

- How does sharing our "hearts" affect you? the community?

How we see ourselves inside determines how and why we do our work with and around others. It is the work of knowing ourselves from the inside out that allows us to work successfully on the outside. Heart maps are a wonderful way to sharpen that inner vision. Enjoy two of our favorite examples (see Figures 5-4 and 5-5 on page 78):

The Wonderful Gift Lesson

What is the first thing that you do when you see a beautifully wrapped gift? Your mind immediately fills with questions: What is inside? Is it for me? Who did this come from? Will I like it? No one had to tell you to start wondering; instinctively questions pour out.

What would reading, learning, and study in math and history look like if students approached these content area texts and ideas with the same vivacious curiosity? Successful!

Great learners approach content study in the same way they do an unwrapped gift. They innately wonder: What is this book about? What do I know about this topic? Will I like it? What will I learn?

Successful content learners

- use curiosity to propel them forward in the text, predicting, and wondering what will come next.

Figure 5-4   Heart Map A

Figure 5-5   Heart Map B

- ask specific questions to guide them toward important ideas. Their questions help them determine importance and interact deeply within and across the text.

- leave the text with more questions than they began with: How does this fit with what I already know? What does this remind me of? Is there more written by this author or about this subject? I wonder if...?

- see texts as "gifts" and use their ability and capacity to question, "unwrap," or "unpack" meaning.

Many of our students see questions as something done *to* them by someone else, *after* reading, and for the purpose of assessment. Unfortunately, this has created a generation of great question answerers but very few proficient question askers. The following gift lesson puts a face on the invisible elements of passion: inquiry and curiosity. Our hope is that students will see books as "gifts" to their minds and upon seeing the text, act accordingly by letting their questions flow.

For readers of all ages, it is ultimately the questions we ask ourselves that make the act of reading personal, exciting, and transformative. If we help to make our students better question askers, we honor passion of the domain and the contributors to it.

To introduce the idea of books as "gifts, you can prepare a large, gift-wrapped box and fill it with a special treat for your students. Arrange for this box to be delivered to your classroom on the first day of the lesson or unit of study. (Hint: The box should look like a really nice gift, with a huge bow that is big, square, and pretty.) Tell the students that this is a special present for them. Get them excited and curious about the contents.

Immediately students will begin to wonder, and the questions will fly! Make sure you have a pen in hand and record their responses:

- What is this?

- What's inside?

- Can we see?

- Who brought this to us?

- Does everyone get one?

- Is it for us...really?

More Ideas to Explore

1. Make your passions public. Find a way to show, display, or demonstrate something you absolutely love about your discipline or favorite topic of study, especially something that you rarely talk about openly.

2. Invite students to share reflections of their passions. Select space on the walls or in the halls to put their "passion print" for all to see.

3. Quotations, quotations, quotations. Successful people talk about passion. Let these inspirational passion quotes illustrate the importance of having passion and drive home the message that being passionate matters:

- "A great leader's courage to fulfill his vision comes from passion, not position." —John Maxwell

- "A strong passion for any object will ensure success, for the desire of the end will point out the means." —William Hazlitt

- "Above all, be true to yourself, and if you cannot put your heart in it, take yourself out of it." —Author Unknown

- "Develop a passion for learning. If you do, you will never cease to grow." —Anthony J. D'Angelo

- "Don't ask yourself what the world needs; ask yourself what makes you come alive. And then go and do that. Because what the world needs is people who have come alive." —Harold Whitman

- "Follow your heart, but be quiet for a while first. Ask questions, then feel the answer. Learn to trust your heart." —Author Unknown

- "Follow your passion, and success will follow you." —Arthur Buddhold

- "Great dancers are not great because of their technique; they are great because of their passion." —Martha Graham

- "If there is no passion in your life, then have you really lived? Find your passion, whatever it may be. Become it, and let it become you and you will find great things happen FOR you, TO you and BECAUSE of you." —T. Alan Armstrong

- "Never underestimate the power of passion."—Eve Sawyer

- "Nothing great in the world has been accomplished without passion." —Georg Wilhelm Friedrich Hegel

- "Passion is in all great searches and is necessary to all creative endeavors." —W. Eugene Smith

- "So try to pursue the very things that you are passionate about—that is the difference between good and great! —Shawn Doyle

- "The more intensely we feel about an idea or a goal, the more assuredly the idea, buried deep in our subconscious, will direct us along the path to its fulfillment." —Earl Nightingale

- "Without passion you don't have energy, without energy you have nothing." —Donald Trump

- "When work, commitment, and pleasure all become one and you reach that deep well where passion lives, nothing is impossible." —Nancy Coey

- "Passion is the genesis of genius." —Anthony Robbins

- "Passion and purpose go hand in hand. When you discover your purpose, you will normally find it's something you're tremendously passionate about." —S. Pavlina

- "Never underestimate the power of passion." —Author unknown

- "There is no passion to be found playing small—in settling for a life that is less than the one you are capable of living." —Nelson Mandela

- "Passion rebuilds the world for the youth. It makes all things alive and significant." —Ralph Waldo Emerson

- "All human actions have one or more of these seven causes: chance, nature, compulsions, habit, reason, passion, desire." —Aristotle

- "Great ambition is the passion of a great character. Those endowed with it may perform very good or very bad acts. All depends on the principles which direct them." —Napoleon Bonaparte

- "With me poetry has not been a purpose, but a passion." —Edgar Allan Poe

Invite students to bring in and share their own quotations.

4. Let Photos Speak. there is nothing that speaks passion like a learner's smiling face. It requires no words or commentary, but is a visual reminder of how good learning feels when you are passionate.

5. Talk Passion Talk. The words we surround ourselves with affect our thoughts and actions. Is your classroom a place where passion is spoken? Do you hear students talking about learning in this way:

WOW! AMAZING! YOU GOTTA SEE/READ/DO THIS! CHECK IT OUT! and let's not forget…THIS ROCKS!!!

Place posters around the room with these passionate reactions and responses to learning, and have students talk about the experiences and artifacts that compelled such emotion.

6. Exhibit Passion Profiles. Our books shelves are filled with inspiration and guidance of passionate individuals. Encourage students to seek out and

identify their own role models and mentors creating a classroom collection for all to use.

7. Take a gallery walk in and out of classrooms when no one is there. Ask your students to step into the classroom for a few seconds and record the first two words they use in describing the experience. Together you can sort and sift through the words, categorizing the attributes of classrooms that made students say "WOW" and characteristics of classrooms that produced a lesser reaction.

If nothing on this list jumps out to you or seems doable, think about the spaces and places you feel most inspired by. Take note or even better, take a picture of the elements of their design. What makes you feel comfortable, safe, willing to share, and motivated there? Think also about the places that dampen your spirit and rob you of energy so you can ensure there is no evidence of such passion-deflators in your classroom. Of course, we want you to ask the students. They may not be able to articulate the intricate details of why they feel excited, but they will certainly give you insight into whether your room, as it is currently organized and arranged, fires their passion.

6

Managing the Clubhouse Classroom

The Clubhouse Classroom is organized chaos

—The Authors

Managing a classroom where students are prepared for hard work takes lots of modeling, guidance, and practice. In this chapter, we will walk you though a three-phase framework that makes it simple to manage the Clubhouse classroom atmosphere so it is filled with students who are passionate about learning.

We have organized the lessons into the three different phases of learning:

♦ Phase One: Launching the Learning—Passion Discovery

♦ Phase Two: Practicing Our Passion:—Learning Is Thinking

♦ Phase Three: Sharing Our Gifts—The Passion Project

The Three Phase framework is designed to meet the following goals:

1. to learn the key roles and routines
2. to set the expectation and groundwork for both independent and interdependent thinking and learning
3. most important, to grow to know your students and help them discover their passions.

It will take time and a gradual release of responsibility so that students act successfully as both independent and interdependent learners. The lessons that follow will give you a sense of how we begin the year in the Clubhouse Classroom with our students.

We hope this gives you a place to start as you craft your own unique conversations with your students. We want you to take our words and adapt these launching lessons and language within each phase to find the just right fit for you. Remember you are the Chief Learning Officer!

Figure 6-1 Daily Schedule Sample

Learning Now Opening	8:45 – 9:00
Boardroom Meeting	9:00 – 9:20
Learning Club Time	9:20 – 10:15
Special Class	10:15 – 10:45
Recess	10:45 – 11:00
Content Area Time	11:00 – 11:30
Content Area Time	11:30 – 12:30
Lunch	12:30 – 12:50
Recess	12:50 – 1:20
Content Area Time	1:20 – 2:15
Recess	2:15 – 2:30
Content Area Time	2:30 – 3:10
Closing	3:10 – 3:20

To assist with planning and to illustrate the big picture in the Passion-Driven Classroom, consult the following charts. The first chart is a sample daily schedule (Figure 6-1). Each section of the chart shows a suggested section of the day in the passion-driven classroom at the elementary school level.

You may have more or less daily blocks, periods, or sections of time for specific content instruction than is indicated on these figures. Depending on your school, grade level, or schedule, you may have more special classes or periods, for example, music, physical education, art, family living, industrial technology, and so on.

The Three Phases In Action

Each of the phases may take several weeks, depending on your learners and the complexity of the lessons within the learning phase. You may want to carry these lessons into the content-specific areas of the day in the beginning of the year to get it all in. See Figure 6-2, The Three Phases At-A-Glance.

Let's recap the routine:

1. The Opening Message Lessons

2. The Boardroom Meetings and Learning Club work that follows

Figure 6-2 The Three Phases At-A-Glance

	Focus	Purpose
PHASE One	Passion Discovery	Defining passion and discovering student passions. Morning routines, Boardroom procedures, and Learning Club work are taught as the C.L.O. models thinking and questioning. Students are introduced to the term "expert," and study the characteristics and behaviors of their expert counterparts.
PHASE Two	Learning Is Thinking	Students learn to recognize their own thinking. Learning is active and requires thinking tools. Students learn about "good fit" tools and start implementing the Thinking Notebook.
PHASE Three	Practicing Our Passion: The Passion Project	The Passion Project is added to the Learning Clubs. Students apply what they have learned in the previous two phases to investigate their own passion in a special Passion Project.

3. Content Area Time: Content Connections

4. The Closing Lessons

Within each of the three Phases of Learning, we give you sample anchor lessons. In the Clubhouse Classroom, an *anchor lesson* is a lesson directed by the Chief Learning Officer that explicitly teaches and models desired learning behaviors. These lessons anchor the procedures, rituals, and learning behaviors for students from which learning builds in the months yet to come. Adapt them as you see fit based on your teaching role.

Phase One:
Launching the Learning—Passion Discovery

A few years back, while we were working in a third-grade classroom, we encountered a very clever group of four boys. These boys had a learning clubs classroom that allowed them to form their own writers and strategy club. Each club member had their own area of expertise. Harry knew how to write computer programs. Bernard and Jason had a deep interest in strategy trading card game. Finally, Joe had an amazing creative streak for illustrating and creating original fantasy creatures. Together, they unleashed their passions by creating their own fantasy video game, collection cards, and strategy game. Things were not always like this for the boys. At the beginning of the school year, they snuck around, passing commercially created trading cards. Each visit to the locker or bathroom meant confiscating a card or note. The teacher found herself ready to literally pull out her hair with this group of boys. It seemed as if all they could do or think about was related to this popular piece of pop culture. Finally, she embraced their passion, helped them connect and discover their passion, and allowed them to practice it. That year, the boys produced a 5-inch-thick binder of their own original strategy trading card game, strategy instructions, diagrams, and to top it all off, an actual video game programmed by Harry. Through this passion-driven project, the boys learned the interpersonal skills of how to work together to problem solve, negotiate, and compromise. They also demonstrated their competency in nonfiction text structures and text features, synthesis, and composition. To practice your passion is to truly learn.

Phase One occurs over the course of the first month of school. The purpose of the first phase of teaching is three-fold. First, it focuses on getting to really know your students. Second, this period offers the time needed for students to get to know themselves. As teachers and students work together to define passion, the students discover their own passions. And finally, students are trained in the essential routines and roles.

The C.L.O. models thinking and questioning in the context of learning about the specific routines and procedures of the Clubhouse Classroom. We introduce the students to the term "expert" and then explicitly teach the Learning Clubs at the end of this phase. Students study the characteristics and behaviors of their expert counterparts. For example, who is a mathematician? What tools do they use? How do they think and work? This is the phase in which students study the attributes of mathematicians, historians, writers, and other desired roles so that they can replicate the same behaviors the rest of the year.

The Opening Message Anchor Lessons

Anchor Lesson: What Is The Opening Message?

In the first phase, the opening message lessons teach students how to be active thinkers about their world, as well as how to articulate their thinking and develop a thinking vocabulary. The teacher thinks aloud daily about how to do this and provides the opportunity for students to practice, too. Thinking aloud models the mental processes needed to work, so eventually it becomes a habit and carries over into work in the Learning Clubs.

The very initial opening messages the first week of school begin with lessons that help students understand the Learning Now! message routine. On large chart paper, a SmartBoard, or on an overhead transparency, a Learning Now! message is displayed from the teacher with something he or she has learned about or thinks is cool or interesting in the world in the past 24 hours. For example, the first messages look and sound like this:

Teacher   Dear Learners, Welcome to a new year! I am so excited to be your teacher this year. I am even more excited to share with you something that I just learned. It is something I really WONDER about. I love things that have to do with space and the universe. Did you know that they are looking for water on the moon? I saw this on the news last night, and then went to read about it online on the NASA website. They even set a bomb off on the moon! I wonder what they will find and if it is a good idea to do this to the moon. What do you think? Write about this and what you think. Do this on a sticky note. Sincerely, Your Chief Learning Officer (a.k.a. your CLO).

This will go on each day of the week, for at least a week. Change this wording with a new example each day.

Anchor Lesson: Thinking During The Opening Message

The teacher varies the metacognitive language used each day in Phase I such as: "I...wonder, predict, think, question, propose, disagree with, agree with, ponder...." You get the idea. The point is to integrate the language of thinking within a context that interests students.

The Boardroom and Learning Club Anchor Lessons

Discovering and sharing passions about Learning Now! is the focus during the first phase. Students also experience the Boardroom meeting concept. Students learn what to do the first minute they step into the room as well as what the Boardroom meeting entails each day and what to do in Learning Clubs after the daily Boardroom meeting. The very beginning lessons are focused on passion discovery as well as teaching students how to work together in a small group. Students specifically experience how to collaborate and listen through these lessons over the time frame of several weeks. We are careful to unleash the students into the classroom all at once. By the end of these weeks, they will have participated in all of the Learning Clubs as well as individually visited with the teacher. They will also learn the procedure of setting an agenda, so that later, they will set their own weekly agendas in their Learning Clubs.

The very first anchor lessons sound and look like the following.

Anchor Lesson: What is Learning Now?

Students bring what they wrote/thought about from Learning Now! message each day.

Teacher   Today/this week we start a new year. The best learners study and question things they know and care about. We call this having a "PASSION" for learning. All of us have a passion for learning, especially learning about our favorite things. Today, you came into the classroom and read a message from me about one of my favorite things. What do you think about this?" (Discussion.) Each morning, we will have a Learning Now! message like this. It will be something that I have learned about in the past 24 hours. We call it Learning Now! because it has JUST HAPPENED, and it something that I am interested in/passionate about as a learner. Each day, you will also think about what you learned now, in the past 24 hours, and get to talk about it. Be ready to share something each day about what you are excited and passionate about as a learner.

Anchor Lesson: Boardroom

To introduce the Boardroom meeting, the teacher explains the reasoning and procedures involved. Far too many mission statements and classroom rules adorn our walls and collect dust. We believe in these promises and want to make sure that our students understand how serious we are about accomplishing the mission of preparing them for the world and the challenges they face. We are so committed to the mission that we are willing to make public for them those beliefs, knowing that failing to deliver on these learning promises will result in loss of attention, decreased motivation, apathy, disengagement, and passionless learning.

Teacher   We have gathered together several times each morning to talk about our learning discoveries. We know that active citizens are aware of the world and its happenings. They also know how to have a discussion with other people about the world they live in. In many clubs and businesses, there is something called a "boardroom meeting." This meeting is held in a special room called "the boardroom." This area of our classroom is our Clubhouse Boardroom. (The teacher shares examples of real companies, preferably local, that have boardroom meetings). This is a time and place where a group of special people, usually a group of leaders in a club, share their thoughts and do their best thinking and discuss important topics. They do this because they care about their work and the club. When we work together, we do our best thinking. Today, we are going to discuss how to take turns sharing what we think about each other's Learning Now! discoveries.

Next, the teacher models by asking two or three volunteers to engage in a discussion about the Learning Now! topics shared. The teacher explains that they are developing a chart that lists their Clubhouse Boardroom Bylaws, a set of rules that helps them do their best thinking in a polite and professional way all year.

Over several lessons, new students are selected for modeling as they discuss and troubleshoot the following:

- How to summarize your point and thinking so that others understand what you are saying

- How to listen (body language, eye contact, and paying attention)

- How to politely disagree with an idea or thought

- What to do when you can't think of anything to say

- How to admit when you are wrong

- How to keep thoughts to yourself and when it's a good time to do so

- Where to find news, for example, TV, websites, newspapers, brochures

Anchor Lesson: Boardroom By-Laws Contract

The following contract is a testament to our commitment. (Feel free to make adaptations as you think about creating something meaningful for you and your students.) Once created, you read aloud and each student has a copy to sign.

Teacher   Welcome to our classroom. This contract represents our mission to create a learning experience that will challenge, engage, and support you to make powerful changes in your lives as learners.

As your teacher, I am 100% committed to your success. I will be an open listener and provide honest feedback. I can serve you best when you communicate openly and freely with me about your needs and your progress.

As a student, you are responsible for ensuring that we are moving in the direction you desire. We will customize your learning path to meet your specific situation and goals. As we construct your unique plan for success, we will incorporate the concepts and principles of passionate learning. Together we will determine realistic assignments and completion dates for them.

You commit to at least 5 to 10 minutes a day to work on your learning plan. Your success is based largely upon how well you accomplish the goals you set and the attitude in which you approach this work and study.

Our time together spans over the next eight months, and each day we learn together will be vital. I am committed to helping you move forward, accomplishing your goals, and seeing you leave this year confident and empowered by who you have become.

In summary, this agreement includes:

Your Commitments

- ♦ Communicate openly.
- ♦ Devote at least 5 to 10 minutes a day to your work/study.
- ♦ Complete all weekly exercises and assignments.
- ♦ Give 110% effort to the process, knowing that mistakes are valued.

My Commitments

- ♦ Be fully excited and prepared for each session.
- ♦ Provide insight, guidance, and accountability.
- ♦ Give open and honest feedback.
- ♦ Customize the program to meet your needs.
- ♦ Keep all communication confidential.

If these terms are in harmony with your expectations and beliefs, please sign, date, and return a copy to me. I promise this will be the best year ever, and I look forward to being your teacher.

Signed: _____
(Sign your name)

The teacher records the class-generated ideas on a chart titled, "Boardroom By-laws." An anchor chart is a collaboratively developed poster that serves as a reminder of procedures and routines. The Boardroom By-laws are displayed for reference all year.

Anchor Lesson: Setting an Agenda

At first, the teacher models what an agenda involves using a real-life example. After that, the teacher and students work together in developing a weekly agenda for one of the Learning Club's work. The teacher uses a large copy of the Club Thinkbook Record. In the lesson here, we use the History Club. During the week that the teacher and students generate the agenda for the Historians, ALL students will be Historians so that they can practice working through the tasks.

In the beginning lessons, as the teacher writes the agenda on large chart paper, on an Interactive Board, or on an overhead, the teacher thinks aloud about the processes and procedures for determining what is important for the week and how to organize the list of tasks. We use a large copy of the Club Record Sheet for each Club. This is posted on large chart paper in each club area. Gradually, the teacher invites student participation and it becomes a shared writing experience in which students and teacher are working together, with the teacher eventually acting as the scribe. Finally, when students are demonstrating independence with this procedure, the teacher has the students set the agendas in their Learning Clubs. They can write their task and agenda on the Club Record sheet in their Club Thinkbooks.

The teacher will want to pull aside the Learning Clubs as a small group and guide them the first few weeks that they are setting their own agendas. A bulletin board, a section of a dry-erase board, or an area of wall space is set aside specifically where each Learning Club posts their weekly agenda. At times, the teacher will want to dictate a task(s) for the Learning Clubs that may have content area connections or relate to something specifically outlined in the curriculum. Or, the task may involve a procedure that they need to refine from the Boardroom By-laws such as, "Take turns this week doing..." or "Work on effective listening...." The lesson introducing how to set an agenda sounds like the following:

Teacher We have all been learning about what happens in our Learning Clubs. You have visited several Learning Clubs already and discovered what can be studied. Now, we will become more focused on what we want to get done in the Learning Clubs. When you tackle a big job or task, it helps to have some ideas how you will start. You think about what you want to do first, and then what comes next. Think about going on a dream vacation. Let's say we want to go to the best water park in the world. How would we start planning? Well, I know that I would have to think about where the best water park in the world is located. At the top of my AGENDA, I am going to write the question or task that I need to answer or complete. Great agendas start with a reason. They start with a question or task that we need to complete. This helps us stay focused on what is important and the job we want to complete. (The teacher writes the question, Where are the best water parks located?) Next, I think about where I need to look and what I need to do to find out the answer to my question. I'm going to write my ideas underneath my question. This is going to be my "to do" list for the week.

The lessons continue in the Boardroom with the teacher modeling what he or she did to work through the agenda. The teacher models how items are checked off as they are completed that week and how tasks can be added. The following week, the teacher bridges this real-life example with the Learning Club Work. This becomes a shared writing experience.

Teacher   You've seen how I worked through my Agenda in planning my dream water park vacation. I had a lot of tasks to complete to prepare for my travels. This week, we will learn how to set an Agenda for our work in Learning Clubs. This week all of us will be Historians. We will all work in the History Club as Historians this week. (This is when the teacher brings in content area work).

In Social Studies, we have been learning about the hardships the pioneers suffered traveling along the Oregon Trail. We know that survival was their goal. Travel has really changed over history…think about my travel plans for my dream vacation! This week, we are going to explore the following question: (The teacher writes this guiding question at the top of the chart paper) How has the experience of travel changed over the past 150 years? This week, it will be our goal to research as Historians how travel has changed. Where will we begin? (Next, the teacher creates a numbered list or bulleted list of steps and things to do as Historians). It will be your job when it is your group's turn to work through our class Agenda as Historians. (Then, as each Boardroom meeting reconvenes each day, a short discussion follows that discusses how the work is going on the Agenda).

Anchor Lesson: Passion Scavenger Hunt

The scavenger hunt's purpose is twofold. First, it gradually introduces students to the Learning Clubs. Only a group of students participate in each Learning Club daily. The following may be broken into two to three lessons, depending on the age and level of independence.

Teacher This year, sometimes we will work alone, and sometimes we will work together in groups and with partners. During Clubtime, it is a time for us to work in groups or partners in our Learning Clubs. We have several Learning Clubs in our classroom. Some of them might really, really interest you, while others may not be so exciting... yet! How will you know when and where to go with your Learning Club? You will know by looking at the Clubtime Schedule. Sometime this week, you will work with a group and complete a passion scavenger hunt AND you will visit with me and talk about yourself and your interests. Even though you are with a group during the scavenger hunt, make sure that you complete your hunt by yourself. Your task is to visit each Learning Club this week and find information on your scavenger hunt. There is also a place for you to rate how much you liked that Club. For example, today it says, "I get to be a Scientist and visit The Lab." I am going to look at my scavenger hunt sheet and do the tasks and look for the information on the sheet at the Lab. I am also going to decide how much I liked this Club. After I have worked in all the Learning Clubs by the end of the week, I will rank them in order. #1 is my favorite and #6 is my least favorite.

Anchor Lesson: Student Interview: What Makes Me ME?

While the students are visiting the workstations this week in the Passion Scavenger Hunt lessons, students are waiting to be interviewed by the teacher. The student interview provides data for the teacher in forming future Learning Club formations. The teacher will study the individual student interviews and student rankings generated by the lessons to form the initial Mathematicians, Scientists, and so on based on their particular interest level rankings as shown in Figure 6-3a on page 95 and Figure 6-3b on page 96, the teacher meets with individuals and completes this interview:

1. How do I describe me?
2. What causes me to smile, laugh, get excited?

3. What captures my attention, gets me interested, makes me want to "stay longer"?

4. What do I always seem to make time for?

5. What occupies my mind even when I do not have time to do it? What do I think about most?

6. What do people notice most about me?

7. When people meet me for the first time, what is the most common thing they say?

8. What words do others use to describe me?

9. What words do I use to describe myself?

10. When I am alone, I almost always...

11. When I am with my friends, we most like to...

12. How am I different from my friends?

13. What makes me unique?

14. What makes me most happy?

Now use these questions to help you answer this one...What makes me ME?

Anchor Lesson: The Talent Profile Interview

This lesson has students interview a partner so that they can use it to draw their partner's Talent Portrait. These portraits will eventually be framed and displayed in the classroom.

Teacher   Your job today during Clubtime is to interview your partner about their talents. You will ask your partner a set of questions called "My Talent Profile." When we work with partners, it is important that we really listen and take note of what the other person is saying. A good listener has eye contact, listens and doesn't interrupt, and take good notes about what their partner is saying, because later you are going to draw a portrait of your partner with the things from the interview worked into the portrait. But for today, your task is to listen and take the best notes possible. (Students could also video tape their partner while asking the questions using flip videos. Later, they can refer back and pause the session while drawing the portraits.)

This information can help you when doing your project research and work. Start with this list of questions and then feel

Figure 6-3a What Makes Me – "ME!"

Name _____Fernando_____

1. How do I describe me?

   Fun. Outgoing. Exciting. Athletic. hard working

2. What causes me to smile, laugh, get excited?

   Friends. Funny Jokes. People I enjoy seeing

3. What captures my attention, gets me interested, makes me want to "stay longer" with a task or experience?

   Building things. something that interests me

4. What do I always seem to make time for?

   Sports. Friends

5. What occupies my mind even when I do not have time to do it? What do I think about most?

   Relaxing. sleeping. pain

6. What do people notice most about me?

   Strong sense of humor.

7. When people meet me for the first time, what is the most common thing they say?

   That im funny + cute

8. What words do others use to describe me?

   Beast. Stud. Funny

9. What words do I use to describe myself?

   Cool. Outgoing. Determined

10. When I am alone, I almost always...

    Relax. Eat. Think. talk to others

11. When I am with my friends, we most like to...

    Play sports. Chill. eat. Explore

12. How am I different than my friends?

    I work hard + Im determined

13. What makes me unique?

    I think differently

14. What makes me most happy?

    Being with my friends in Piece. Iowa Football Games

Figure 6-3b   What Makes Me – "ME!"

Name _____ katlyn _____

1. How do I describe me?

 I would say I am someone that likes to have fun with the people closest to me.

2. What causes me to laugh, smile, get excited?

 When I am by people I love and watching scary movies.

3. What captures my attention, gets me interested, makes me want to "stay longer" with a task or experience?

 Exiting games and big events

4. What do I always seem to make time for?

 friends and family

5. What occupies my mind even when I do not have time to do it? What do I think about most?

 Getting a job in the future and having a family when I grow up.

6. What do people notice most about me?

 Im blond

7. When people meet me for the first time, what is the most common thing they say?

 Weird not ugly but no pretty

8. What words do others use to describe me?

 Weird loud funny.

9. What words do I use to describe myself?

 abnormal smart.

10. When I am alone, I almost always…

 Read watch T.V. or go on facebook.

11. When I am with my friends, we most like to…

 Hang out and go to the mall and the pool roller skating and other fun stuff!

12. How am I different than my friends?

 not in advants classes better at sports.

13. What makes me unique?

 I can spread my toe all apart!

14. What makes me most happy?

 Being with the people that don t anoy me and love me.

free to add your own discoveries. Answer the questions as best as you can. Remember, some of our best talents are hidden.

The Talent Profile Lesson provides the opportunity for every student to identify those things for which they have some area of expertise or talent. It is one of the very first exercises to bring out the individual student's passions. It is this lesson that the teacher can begin to truly get to know each and every person in their classroom. See examples in Figures 6-4 and 6-5.

You read over the interview questions and explain each one.

A. Your Knowledge: What do you know a lot about?

Your knowledge may be about anything and can come from any source. Examples: animals, sports, musical instruments, history, building or creating something, surviving a difficult time, handling a sickness or disease, secrets to being healthy/happy, making others happy

B. Your Skills: What do you know how to do well?

These may include skills developed and used at work, around the house, in sports or games, at your hobbies or recreational activities, or in anything else that you do. Examples: training, experiments, competing or being a competitor, reading well, studying, new technology, video games, taking care of someone or something

C. Your Strengths: What are you best known for?

When people describe you, they say you are good at _____. Examples: "I'm very disciplined." "I am always positive and happy." "I always make people feel _____." "I am careful." "I can really be trusted." "I am not afraid to say what I am thinking."

D. Your Abilities: What kinds of things do you believe you have a talent for?

Examples: "I have the ability to organize things." "I have the ability to get my friends and family motivated." "I am good at fixing things." "People tell me that I have a really good _____."

E. Your Interests: What kinds of things do you LOVE to do?

What have you dreamed of doing if you had the chance? Examples: "I have always dreamed of _____." "I really would love to try _____." "I have never _____, but I would love to _____."

F. Your Experience: What kinds of things have you seen and done in your life?

Our personal experiences not only shape what we know, they can shape who we are and who we may become. Even if the experiences we have may be ones that we do not wish to repeat, EVERY experience is an important learning

Figure 6-4 Talent Profile (Andrew)

My Talent Profile: _Andrew_   Interviewed by: _Chuck_

1. What do you know a lot about?
   I know a lote about baseball and math.

2. What do you know how to do well?
   I know how to do hitting well.

3. What are you best known for?
   I am funny.

4. What kinds of things do you believe you have a talent for?
   Baseball, math,

5. What kinds of things do you LOVE to do?
   My interests are skydiving, going to a major sport of some sort.

6. What kinds of things have you seen and done in your life?:
   Cello, baseball, flying in a plane a lot.

7. What can you share with others?
   I like to listen to music.

---

tool. Think about what you have experienced that could be used to help you this year in your work. What experiences were the most exciting? most difficult? remarkable? What have you done that you might want to build on?

Examples: "I traveled to another country." "I have met someone who _____." "I played the piano for five years _____." "I was a part of a club _____." I tried something scary and I learned to _____." "I volunteered."

G. What can you share with others?

If there is any other kind of information you want to add, add it here, such as things that we might not have explored. Feel free to write or draw anything that comes to mind and do not worry how it fits in. Many of the the categories overlap. Remember our goal is to discover and uncover ALL your hidden talents.

The Talent Portrait

For this important work, the teacher can play inspiring or grand music in the background to set the tone during this lesson. See to figure 6-6 on page 100.

Figure 6-5 Talent Profile (JaQuan)

My Talent Profile ___JaQuan___   Interviewed by: ___Chad___

1. *What do you know a lot about?*
   Playing Baseball

2. *What do you know how to do well?*
   Making my bat hit the ball

3. *What are you best known for?*
   Being small Being good at math

4. *What kinds of things do you believe you have a talent for?*
   Playing baseball

5. *Your interests:*
   Listing to music. playing on the computer
   Play on a allstar baseball team

6. *Your experience:*
   Won a medal in baseball   Not having a winning recored in baseball

7. *You share:*
   Like to play football

Teacher   Today, we are going to start our Talent Portraits. Portraits are drawings of a person, usually the face. In a moment, you will get with the partner I assigned to you for the Talent Profile. You have all completed your Talent Profile interview about your passions and talents. You already shared with a partner those things that you know most about and care about.

Now, you are going to draw a portrait of your partner. You will want to read their profile again before you begin to draw. You will sit face-to-face, across from your partner. You will draw their portrait, including details from their profile. This is where you can get creative. For example, if I told my partner that I loved golfing, they might choose to draw a golf course in the background behind my head. If they learned that I love dogs, they might give me a necklace with a dog shape on it. If my favorite team was the Green Bay Packers, perhaps they would put me in a yellow and green sweatshirt

Figure 6-6   Talent Portrait

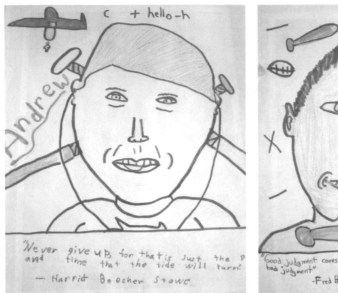

or stocking cap. Remember, portraits are drawings of the shoulders and head. You will notice that there is blank space at the bottom (show example). This is a place for you to write your favorite quote. Your favorite quote is the only thing that you will draw/write on your own portrait; otherwise, your partner is doing all of the drawing. You will record your quote last, and make sure you give credit by including the name of the person quoted.

When the Talent Portraits are completed, remember to frame them in colorful or gold shiny frames. Gold or metallic spray paint works great to revamp old or inexpensive frames. Display the portraits all year.

Learning Clubs: Bringing It All Together

"How can we expect to train the next generation of scientists if we are not training them to do what scientists actually do?" writes Dan Willingham (2009, p. 127). "This sounds sensible, even insightful," says Willingham, but, he acknowledges, getting students to engage deeply in content area work requires more than knowing facts and remembering details. Experts see their discipline differently. They think, act, speak, view, and behave differently. The work in the Clubhouse Classroom, and specifically when students engage in the Learning Clubs routine, intentionally mirrors the way scientists, historians, writers and mathematicians do their work.

After all, even the greatest, most passionate scientists did not think like experts when they first started out. They thought and acted like novices. We want students to understand that accomplished mathematicians, scientists, and historians have worked in their field for years, and the knowledge and experience they have accumulated enables them to think and behave in ways that are not open to the rest of us.

The ending Boardroom lessons and Club Work of Phase One focus specifically on the Learning Clubs. Whatever clubs you create and however you label them, these are the lessons that teach both the WHO and the WHAT:

- Who is a Scientist? What does the Science Club do?

- Who is a Geographer? What does the Geography Club do?

- Who is a Mathematician? What does the Math Club do?

- Who is a Journalist/Writer? What does the Writers' Club do?

- Who is a Historian? What does the History Club do?

Learning Club Procedure—Steps 1–4

Each of the Learning Clubs are taught following a specific procedure. The teacher leads the students through each of the Club roles and focuses on

- what the experts DO

- what TOOLS they use

- WHERE they do their work

- WHERE the students will practice the role of the Club

We outline this procedure using the Science Club as an example. You will adapt this procedure for each of the Learning Clubs:

Step 1: Who Is a Scientist?

The teacher starts a conversation about the Science content work they are currently studying in class. For example, if inventions are being studied, then the teacher introduces some famous inventors and their inventions. The class engages in a conversation about famous inventors and how they are scientists. The teacher begins filling out the Anchor Chart.

Step 2: Anchor Chart Quadrant – WHO

Anchor charts are important to the work of the Learning Clubs. Anchor charts are developed and posted in the club work areas of the classroom all

Figure 6-7   Four Quandrant Anchor Chart for a Scientist

A Scientist	
WHO ♦ Inventor 　- George Washington Carver, 　　agricultural chemist	WHAT ♦ Ask questions ♦ Curious about the world ♦ Study their passion
TOOLS ♦ Magnifying glass ♦ Syringe	WHERE ♦ Home ♦ Garage ♦ A lab ♦ University

year. The teacher adds to the chart as they work through the steps that introduce the Learning Clubs. The anchor charts are divided into four quadrants: WHO is a scientist, WHAT scientists Do, scientist TOOLS, and WHERE scientists work. (For our Science Club example, the teacher would write the label WHO in the first quadrant with the word INVENTOR and the scientists' names listed below.) The teacher leaves room in each of the quadrants so that more information can be added as students make discoveries throughout the year, adding examples for each of the quadrants. See Figure 6-7.

Step 3: Anchor Chart Quadrant – WHAT & TOOLS

For this lesson, both the WHAT and the TOOLS are discussed. WHAT do scientists do and What TOOLS do scientists use? Again, using the current Science curriculum and area of study, the teacher engages the class in a discussion about WHAT scientists do, and what TOOLS the scientists use. The class investigates the kind of thinking and tools that scientists use and adds their findings to the anchor chart in the second quadrant labeled TOOLS. For example, scientists ask questions, are curious about the world and how it works, they study their passions, and so on. The students are challenged with the task of finding out what scientists do and what tools they use. The teacher gathers a collection of artifacts that the particular kind of scientist

Figure 6-8   Student-Scientist

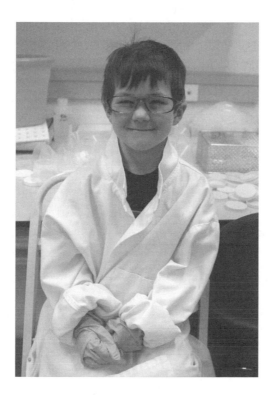

uses and puts them on a tray or display in the classroom. The teacher takes photos of students dressed as scientists holding some tools of the scientist to help students connect with the role as shown in figure 6-8.

Step 4: Anchor Chart Quadrant – WHERE?

WHERE do Scientists work? WHERE will WE work?

Finally, the students and teacher engage in a discussion about WHERE the particular scientist may work. Where would an inventor work? As students discover these answers, they are added under the word WHERE on the last quadrant. An inventor could work in their home or garage. An inventor may work in a lab under very certain controlled conditions. Explain the areas in the classroom where the Science Club will work as scientists, using the classroom TOOLS of scientists.

Each Learning Club is introduced following this procedure until Anchor charts are posted in each of the Learning Clubs. The materials will change depending on what is being studied explicitly in the content areas. We have listed some examples below and ideas for lessons to launch the specific Learning Clubs.

The History Club

Club Description: Students must have a chance not only to explore the world but also to know the world. We want students to understand what history is—beyond the traditional collection of facts and dates. Too often our understanding of other cultures and countries is limited to holiday customs and foods. As students study other parts of the world, we should strive to personalize and humanize learning by making direct connections with others of cultural contexts different from our own. The time in the History Club gives students opportunities to know students from other countries, to learn how background and culture has major implications, to broaden perspectives, and to develop attributes of global citizenship.

Definition of a Historian: Historians study events and happenings of the past and record their questions, discoveries, and answers. They organize their findings so that others can learn from their findings.

Setting up the Archives:

♦ Club Thinkbooks from previous years

♦ maps

♦ reference materials

♦ documentaries

♦ magazines

♦ History Club Thinkbook

♦ graphic Organizers: timelines, blank maps

Thanks to a revolution in technology and communications, our world is more interconnected and interdependent than ever before in human history. Bringing together learners of diverse national origins or cultural backgrounds enriches the learning experience for everyone, improving our understanding of common subjects. Our goal is not only to interest children in learning about history and the cultures different from their own, but also to

♦ better understand their own culture and how it has shaped them.

♦ begin to understand the perspectives of other cultures, leading to increased respect for those who are different from them—in the classroom and throughout the world.

♦ obtain an increased awareness of the value and practicality of social service within and beyond the bounds of schools. The understanding of culture facilitates living with and understanding others of different backgrounds—within the classroom, in the local community, and on the worldwide scale of political, social, and economic interaction.

The Math Club

Club Description: How can we make math come alive for students? Many students thrive with numbers and problem solving, and just as many struggle with math. Making math real and alive helps differentiate the learning for all students as they act as apprentice-mathematicians.

Definition of a Mathematician: Mathematics is an established area of study. Mathematicians come of up with new ways of solving problems as well as solve practical issues in the world of business, engineering, and government, for example.

Setting up the Math Lab: Mathematicians need a comfortable environment to do their best thinking. To start the year, include the following:

♦ Dry-erase boards

♦ Chart tablet

♦ Manipulatives related to the first areas of math study in the content areas

♦ Calculators

♦ Number line

♦ Multiplication/division table

♦ Rulers, compass, protractor

♦ Digital tools on an ipod touch®

♦ 3 Dimensional models of shapes

♦ Real coin sets

The Geography Club

Club Description: The Geography Club wonders about the earth and its features, how these features create regions very different from one another, like jungles and deserts, and the effect of these features on each other and on human societies and culture. Club members can be charged with the task of physically representing what is being studied in class, such as models of earth's physical features and maps.

Definition of a Geographer: The Greek scholar Eratosthenes is known to be the first to use the term "geography," meaning "earth surveyor." A geographer is a scientist who studies and measures the physical features of the earth, such as mountains; rivers, lakes, and oceans; climate; soil and so on to better understand them and how they affect one another, and also the relationship between them and human activity. A geographer might want to know, for example, how glaciers change over time, or how glaciers affect human societies.

Setting up the Maps and Geography Tools in the Archives:

- GlobeWorld and state maps

- digital maps and tools

- cartograms

- surveys

- special purpose maps related to Social Studies content area of study at the time

- Geography Club Thinkbook

The Journalists/Writers' Club

Club Description: This club can have a variety of purposes related to reading and writing. It can serve as the Writing Workshop Hub, where students work on individual pieces of writing and help each other write and edit. It can serve as the place where students submit book recommendations and pieces of writing for class publication. This group can manage the logistics of these tasks. Also, the journalists can do much of the writing and scribing for the class in the daily Boardroom meeting. They can keep an ongoing log of events and happenings and can publish a class newsletter.

Definition of a Writer: Do you consider yourself a writer? Did you know that writing is thinking? How often do you write in a day? What helps you improve, break through writer's blocks, improve your message? These are questions we explore in the Journalist Club. Our goal is to help young writers understand the importance of writing in learning and in their daily lives.

One of the most startling shortcomings of our current education system is the lack of relevant reading. We ask students to read ancient texts that are often difficult to understand and relate to. Rather than helping students relate universal themes to their own lives, we spend time in reading class answering predetermined questions, defining vocabulary words, and completing irrelevant and sometimes even ridiculous tasks—cutting, pasteing, and boring our students right out of the door of the literacy club.

We are not suggesting that we abandon classic texts, or not grapple with the language of Shakespeare. But our top priority must be to instill a passion for literacy.

When readers and writers meet, we want them to understand that

- Reading and writing is a privilege.

- Reading and writing is transformative.

- Reading and writing are not about analyzing plot structure, diagramming sentences, and memorizing events.

- Reading and writing are about enlightenment, engagement, and transformation.

Setting up the Library/Writing Area for the Journalists/Writers:

- books organized by genre and/or author and/or topic

- magazines

- newspapers

- Kindles

- book recommendation cards

- paper of all kinds

- sticky notes

- pens, paper, correction tape or fluid

- Journalist Thinkbook

Where reading and writing happens matters. Most school literacy tasks take place in sterile, cold, and impersonal spaces. Contrast this environment with a Barnes & Noble bookstore. Are the desks in rows, books displayed with covers hidden, the selection limited to one genre? A warm and inviting environment, with natural light and comfortable seating, is beyond warm and fuzzy. It is necessary. When we ask people where they have experienced their most significant conversations, nearly everyone recalls sitting around a kitchen or diningroom table. There is an easy intimacy when gathering at a small table that most of us immediately recognize. When you walk into a room and see it filled with café tables, you expect to be more engaged than you would in a typical business environment.

The Science Club

Club Description: The class Scientists are closely connected to the science content study. They take care of the maintenance and study of the current curricular focus. For example, if the class is studying life sciences, they maintain the habitat and care of the life science being studied. They take careful lab notes and share findings at the Boardroom meetings.

Definition of a Scientist: Scientists are people who are curious about why and how things happen. They are trained to observe and measure phenomena using not only their senses but also tools and complex instruments. Scientists ask questions and then pose answers or theories to answer those questions. Then they test their theories, record the results, and decide if their questions were answered, or perhaps they discovered something they never knew before. They use the "scientific method" to search for answers to their questions. Scientist publish their results so others can know what they discovered and how they did it.

Setting up the Science Lab: Depending on what is being studied, tools might include:

- ◆ magnifying glasses
- ◆ eye droppers
- ◆ petri dishes
- ◆ terrarium
- ◆ spray bottles
- ◆ Science Club Thinkbook

At the end of every day, during Phase One of our Learning Club Framework, we want students to engage in reflective thinking about what they have discovered and practice goal setting for the next day's work.

Phase Two:
Practicing Our Passion—Learning Is Thinking

This phase of learning takes more time as lessons shift away from the routines and procedures and focus heavily instead on metacognition (thinking about one's own thinking). Depending on the independence level of your students, this phase may take at least eight weeks of instruction and practice. Remember that we are "going slow so that we can go fast later."

The purpose of the second phase in launching learning clubs is to help students learn to recognize their own thinking. We teach them that learning is active and requires thinking tools. Students learn about "good fit" tools and start implementing The Thinking Notebook.

The Opening Message Anchor Lessons

Cool & Amazing Quotes!

You can include a new cool and amazing quote each day over several days. Introduce this lesson this way.

Teacher   Dear Thinkers, Good morning, awesome thinkers! Did you know that you are an awesome thinker? All of us love to think, we just like to think about different things. Did you know that I write in a Thinking Notebook? I call it my Thinkbook. I like to collect cool and amazing quotes from famous people. Part of our Opening Message can be about cool and amazing quotes we hear or read from famous people. We can learn a lot from these quotes. One of my favorite quotes is from Abraham Lincoln, "A house divided against itself cannot stand." What do you think this means? Is it about houses? You have a few quotes on your desk by some famous people. Choose your favorite one and be ready to say what you think it means and why you chose it.

Current Events and the World of Journalism

Modify the current event each day. Use the Internet and paper copy of the news as examples.

Teacher   Dear Class, Did you read in the newspaper what happened last night? (Include appropriate example for your age/grade here). I like to read the newspaper for current events. We get a paper copy of the newspaper at home and at school. You learn a lot about current happenings in the newspaper. I also like to read the news on the Web. You can read almost the exact same information at the website on the computer. Copy our local newspaper website in your Thinkbooks. Go to your Journalism section and write it under the websites column (include website here). We will discuss this website and my "current event" at today's Boardroom meeting. (If you have one-to-one laptops or iPods, have the students "bookmark it" or show them at the Boardroom meeting how to do this).

The Boardroom and Learning Club Anchor Lessons

Anchor Lesson: Show Your Thinking—Cool and Amazing Quotes

Teacher   One way people show their thinking is through quotes. This week during Clubtime, you will visit both the Journalists/Writers' workstation and the Historians' workstation. There, you will find cool and amazing quote books and websites. Your job is to write down some favorite quotes and the people who said them. Write them in your Journalist section of your Thinkbook, or if you think it should go in the Historian's section, you may write it there. For example, my quote by Abraham Lincoln would probably go in the Historian's section because this quote was about something really important that happened in history. You might use your favorite quotes later this year in some writing, a research topic, or maybe you will just collect them because you like them.

Anchor Lesson: Introducing the Learner's Thinkbook

Teacher   Boys and Girls, One of the things that I discovered in my studies of successful and passionate learners is that many kept a notebook or journal detailing their thinking and learning life. I have been keeping a Learning Thinkbook for the past five years, and I would like to share it with you today. It has become an important tool in the work that I do. One section has a collection of my favorite cool and amazing quotes. Sometimes I use them in my writing, and sometimes I just like to think about them and what they mean to my life. (Share one or two with the students, explain the Abraham Lincoln quote and its historical significance). Leonardo da Vinci (artist), Charles Darwin (scientist), and Dylan Thomas (poet)—and the thousands of others leading their fields all kept notebooks of thoughts.

These great scholars, artists, and scientists did not write about their thinking because they wanted more records or enjoyed paperwork. They used writing as a powerful tool to increase their knowledge, productivity, and expertise. For today's scientists, designers, entrepreneurs, historians, authors, artists, architects, choreographers, and explorers, writing is a most important instrument and a treasured possession. This Learning Thinkbook, as we will call it, is more than just a notepad or diary; it is a record of their work and their thinking—a place to collect ideas and plans, a place for self-reflection of their work as learners, a place to treasure the strategies and techniques that make them most successful.

You are going to keep a Learning Thinkbook yourself. There is not one way to record your thoughts and plans. Imagine the Thinkbook as a planning book; a place that holds all the activities you wish to pursue. It will also be a record of what you do, what you decide to change, and what you learn when you put your plan into action. This week, we will practice gathering cool and amazing quotes in our Journalist or Historian section.

Your Thinkbook will be the special place where you study the process that you followed as you worked through your workstations and Passion Project, and where you study yourself as a performer. Your thinkbook is the companion that you talk to at any time about what you are thinking and doing. This is a place to record your special interests, thoughts, and ideas. The Learning Thinkbook is always waiting to hear your latest thoughts; no matter how small.

Taking action on ideas and dreams takes courage and perseverance. Anyone can be excited, but few are truly passionate. Few are able to take that exciting idea and take action on it. The information and ideas that you will collect will be the energy and knowledge you need to pursue your project. For the next several days, you will be searching and looking for cool and amazing quotes. Be ready to share them at our Boardroom meetings.

What Is a Current Event?

(For this lesson set, you will need a projector/computer/interactive board for the Boardroom lessons. Each lesson will feature a specific genre in the World of Journalism as a source for Learning Now material. Adapt the script for each genre.)

Project the article. Briefly discuss the current event from the morning message, and what it means in the students' community/world. Highlight the following kinds of articles to fit the Learning Clubs:

A. A current event article about Science

B. A current event article about Mathematics

C. A current event article about History or a new discovery that may change history.

D. A current event article about the Environment/Geography

Bring It All Together Lessons—Learning Club Tools

The last lessons in Phase Two bring it all together with the tools of the trade. Students learn about the tools available to them in the classroom that assist them in their learning. We are passionate learners, and there are indispensable tools that we use to manage our learning lives. We want students to get a look inside of our "learning lifestyle," examine the tools we use, and create their own toolbox as they get to know themselves as learners. As tools are added to the classroom or as you introduce them, you may come back to these lessons. For example, you will want to start with a few core tools to end Phase Two, and then continue teaching the tools throughout the year.

Stuff for the Hands, Head and Heart

Teacher We are passionate learners, and there are indispensable tools that we use to manage our learning lives. We want to get a look inside of our "learning lifestyle", examine the tools we use, and create our own toolboxes for learning. We are going to make a chart this week of all the tools we can use to help ourselves learn. We will discover stuff for our hands, stuff for our heads, and stuff for our hearts.

(The teacher continues to introduce the tools gradually in the Boardroom Lessons, showing them how they can help them work in their specific Learning Clubs).

1. Stuff for Hands:
   - Laptop
   - Cell Phone or other Mobile Device
   - Digital Recorder: Inspiration often strikes in the car or other places or times when a pen and a learner's journal aren't convenient to use. So carry an MP3 recorder or tape recorder.
   - Ipod
   - Recorded Books
   - Flip Video
   - Pen and Paper

2. Stuff for Minds: These tools help us collect and organize our thoughts, become more mindful, and do our work with more precision.
   - Delicious
   - Google Reader
   - Twitter
   - Books: *Five Minds of the Future, Mindset, Outliers, The Innovators Dilemna, Think Like A Genius, The Creative Wack Pack*

3. Stuff for Hearts: These tools and resources keep our hearts full beating with inspiration and energy.
   - Recorded Books
   - TED Talks-live lectures from the worlds most brilliant minds
   - iTunes UClassroom
   - 2.0- Our place to connect

These tools can be introduced in Boardroom lessons that look and sound like the following:

Magazines and Periodicals

Teacher Today's Boardroom meeting is focused on using magazines and periodicals to help us learn about _____. In your Learning Clubs, remember to use the print resources to build upon the information you have already gathered about your topics.

Using models from each of the learning clubs, demonstrate how, as readers, we make use of the different texts to support learning. Encourage students to use the print materials along with the digital resources to expand their learning. Ask students to review material and learning over the past couple of Boardroom sessions. Gather student responses to the following questions:

Teacher What have we already learned about our topic that we didn't know before we began? What questions do we still have about our topic? How will you answer these questions at our next session? How have you been working together as a group?

The Critical Resource: Books

Teacher Today we are going to talk about books, how they can help us learn, and the best ways to explore them. Let's think about this book as an example. (Hold up book with cover and title showing.) What kind of questions do you think a book like this might answer?

Record questions or key ideas students generate. Then model how to use a table of contents and an index to further identify information and help focus inquiry.

Teacher As you use the books and print resources in your Learning Clubs, notice how they add to the information you already knew. Be sure to add to and revise the information in your thinking notebooks.

Blogging and Logging Our Learning

Explain to students that the focus of today's class meeting is on how we synthesize the tools shared at each session to make meaning, and how we use these multimodal resources to demonstrate understanding.

Teacher	One way people share learning is by using a learning blog or a log. Think about your audience, the people who are going to read what you have written. Will they understand what you have written? Why or why not? How can you organize what you have written so that others will understand? Think about how you are going to use your blogs or learning logs to create a place where others can learn about a specific topic. How are you going to synthesize the information you have learned so that others can understand their topic of investigation?

Announce that you will circulate around the room during Club work. As you meet with different Clubs, ask the students to revisit the questions/ideas posed in the Boardroom meeting or on the weekly agenda, as a tool for organizing their ideas. Organization will vary according to the topic and task.

Teacher	Today in your Learning Clubs you will revise and add to your learning blog or log so that others in our class can read and learn from it.

Encourage them to make this interactive. For example, you can invite students to post questions or embed links for readers of their blogs. If students are using logs, invite them to use sticky notes to offer a place for other students to respond to their work.

Blurring the Lines: An Interactive, Multimodal Learning Fair

Teacher	Today's Learning Club work is for a demonstration of learning using the multimodal tools built throughout the learning process. You will have the opportunity to interact with each of the Learning Clubs' blogs or logs. (The nature of the interaction will be guided by the presentation of the information and the decisions the groups make about presentation.) You will have 10 minutes to explore each log. Talk about what you learn from each one. Before you move to the next station, you should write down or post something you learned during the visit and something you would still like to know. Don't forget to compliment each other for good work.

Closing Phase Two

The close of each day is simple and done with purpose. Like professional learners, we use this time together to reflect on what has been accomplished, set goals for tomorrow's works, and brainstorm strategies and techniques to improve our productivity.

Phase Three:
Sharing Our Gifts—The Passion Project

What would you do if your boss gave you free time to do anything you wanted for two hours every week? The only catch is that it would need to benefit others. Would you hug him/her? How would it affect your productivity, level of engagement, and your thoughts and perceptions? That's exactly what your boss would say and do if you were an employee at Google! It's called "The 20 Percent Project" and has become one of the reasons Google has topped the list of FORTUNE Magazine's "100 Best Companies to Work For" for several years running. Employee "free-time" is built into the regular work week at Google.

Here's how it works. Each week, Google engineers work four days on their assigned jobs and projects, with one day per week devoted to pursuing their own special projects with full access to the resources and support of Google. Google's rationale for the project is both simple and profound. Give the proper tools to a group of people who want to make a difference, and they will do just that. Google believes that people work better when they're involved in something they're passionate about. The 20 Percent Projects have resulted in some of Google's most innovative and profitable ideas. Google Maps, Google Labs, Google docs, and Google's latest revolution, Google Wave, are all a direct result of 20 Percent Projects.

Google's founder and CEO, Eric Schmidt, talks about the Google Philosophy:

> "At Google, we know that every employee has something important to say, and that every employee is integral to our success. Googlers thrive in small, focused teams and high-energy environments, believe in the ability of technology to change the world, and are as passionate about their lives as they are about their work. We take great care in how we attract and hire the very best talent—because at Google, people are our most important asset."

The Google Way

We were so inspired by the "Google Way" that we decided to integrate this element into the Clubhouse Classroom. What if our students were given that same respect and trust Google gives its engineers? What would happen if each week, students were given the time, resources, and opportunity to pursue what they were most passionate about? What if EVERY student understood how their talent, passion, and uniqueness was their most valuable asset? What would that mean for their productivity, level of engagement, and thoughts and perceptions about learning and school?

After all, through the first two phases of launching the learning in the Clubhouse Classroom, we have made it a "mission" that school will be a place where students

- ♦ will be prepared for a complex, global world
- ♦ will be able to express themselves, discover their joys, and pursue their passions
- ♦ will progressively take more responsibility for themselves and their education
- ♦ will receive help and support necessary to explore and expand their interests and to discover their talents

Indeed, these goals are lofty. When exactly does this happen? Beyond kindergarten, when do we provide students time to independently explore a current or potential passion while giving them maximum responsibility for their own learning?

Yet it is in longer term, creative work, done either individually or collectively, which combines investigating the topic and presenting it in written form that develops and nurtures the very ideals and competencies to which we aspire.

Phase Three, then, is the independent practice phase of passion-driven learning. It is the time when the teacher is not involved except as a guide and coach to help the student move forward in pursuit of their passion. What do you think happened when we told 28 students that they would have a regular time, opportunity, and the resources to pursue most any topic they wanted to investigate, in any way they wanted, with the only expectation is that the work benefited other learners....SILENCE! We were hoping for hugs, but instead we got looks of confusion, hesitation, even distrust. Responses like....When is this due? Do we have to turn in a report? How will this be graded? How long does it have to be? Will we have to present in front of the class? These responses were powerful illustrations that in spite of good intentions, "school" has not traditionally been the place where passions are pursued.

The Passion Project

The Passion Project day differs from traditional project and Learning Club work in several ways. It synthesizes and applies what habits and behaviors students have developed up to this point working in the Learning Clubs:

1. Passion Projects are continuous: Students were familiar with project work, but many saw projects as something "special" or "different"; something to work on after the "real school work is done." It is important that students see the pursuit of passion as a routine, a standard operating procedure as common as math facts and daily reading.

2. Passion Projects are personal: It is fairly common practice for project-based learning to be related to specific content area objectives, such as a culmination of a unit of study, book, or content exploration. Although many students will be motivated and excited to take class explorations to a more personal level, we wanted to give students freedom to pursue any topic.

3. Passion Projects are unbounded by curriculum: These are separate investigations, commitments to WHATEVER students are passionate about in WHATEVER way they choose to pursue that work. The only "requirement" is that the work will in someway benefit another learner or the community of learners as a whole.

4. Passion Projects are student-driven: Most project work we see is top-down, that is, the teacher controls when the project happens, how long it extends, what the "final product" may look like, and so on.

   The Passion Project works from a different premise. Rather than be handed elaborate thematic units prefabricated by the adults, students must be afforded the opportunity and support to formulate not only the course of study but also the outcomes or standards that inform those lessons. Students decide how, when, and in what way they will be turning their passion work into something that will benefit another.

We introduce this element of Clubhouse Learning when the first two phases are secure. Before students can immerse themselves into a Passion Project, they must be able to work independently as well as interdependently and operate within the Clubhouse Classroom parameters. Certain individual students or groups of students may be able to move more quickly into a Passion Project during the first couple phases of instruction, however, it is important that ALL students are provided the opportunity to investigate something of extreme interest. The very first Passion Project work is launched by immersing the student in the project for a week. Eventually, it will only take place once a week and replace Learning Clubs that day.

Passion Projects work well on early dismissal days and can take the place of a middle school or high school study hall. They can also fit the requirements of a guidance lesson and standards as students are working on something personal and worthwhile to the community or world. The scheduling possibilities are there, we just need to be creative and cognizant of how time is organized for our students each week.

Instead of the Google Project, we've got the Passion Project! Wait until you see what kids can do!

The Opening Message Lessons:

In the opening messages of the first week introducing the Passion Project, we must ensure that students understand our full intention and purpose behind the Passion Project. The first lessons follow a script mirroring the Google Project:

Imagine the Possibilities

Teacher   Dear Students, What would you do if I gave you study time to do anything you wanted for two hours every week? The only catch is that It would need to benefit others. This week, something very exciting is going to happen in our Clubhouse Classroom. To get started, think about your Passion Portrait. What are you really curious about? Be ready to share what you would study and do with two hours of free time in our classroom.

Early Passion Project Work

Teacher   Good Morning, Friends. This is your chance to finally investigate something that YOU are interested in. For some of you, this will be your first opportunity to actually research something you care about. We do not want waste the opportunity! This morning, you may go right to your Passion Project. Be ready to share what you are studying and doing at today's Boardroom Meeting.

The Boardroom Lessons & Passion Project Work:

Heart Wonders

Teacher   Your Passion Project does not replace Learning Clubs, except for this day of the week. It is not a substitution for important content area work. We know how to research, think, and discuss our learning. On Passion Project day, we will use our Heart Maps to ignite our research. Most days of the week, you are working in Learning Clubs on "Research Wonders." Research Wonders are questions about things that you can hold in your head and hand. On Passion Project day, we will work on "Heart Wonders," which are those questions that are about what's in your heart and mind.

Heart Wonders are the big, pondering, and sometimes personal questions that we ask ourselves such as: What will my future be? What makes a friend? Why do bad things sometimes happen to people? These questions are meant to be pondered, savored, and explored by reflecting on them but also by having a conversation with another person; they are not necessarily researched in the same way as more informational questions.

Early Passion Project Work

Teacher This morning, you read in the Opening Message that you could go right to your Passion Project work. Turn to your neighbor and share with them what you are studying and why you chose it. Finally, tell them the next thing you will do when you go back to your Passion Project. (Students share with the person next to them the area and topic they are passionate about and currently studying.)

Tools for Sharing Our Passion

Blogging Our Passions

Blogging is more than a hobby; it is a passion of ours. When we began reading and writing blogs, we were unsure of what to expect. We imagined blogs to be a public diary or a space for individuals to share what they had been up to lately. Our eyes were soon opened to the fact that bloggers were searching for and sharing their passions. As we read the blogs of others, we knew "something" was inspiring these individuals to write about their specific topics.

Having a place to share with the world what you are most passionate about not only changes *how* you write, it changes *who* you are—and that is before any comments. When others begin to respond to your thoughts and ideas, the passion becomes even more intense. The act of committing every day, or at least on a consistent basis, to talking about, researching, and sharing your passion leads to productivity. Some actions may be small—a comment, a resource, an image to match your thoughts—but many conversations have led to groups of passionate people connecting and collaborating.

When we look at why we blog, what we blog about, and which posts of others stir something within us, we find ourselves closer to identifying our passion. We wanted students to experience this transformative process first-hand.

The Passion Project Blog enables students to

1. identify and make public their gifts and talents
2. find and connect with others who share the same
3. explore how they want to give the gifts to others via writing, performing, selling, creating, designing, planning, teaching

As part of the Passion Project, students are asked to contribute to a class blog where they have an opportunity to share their passions, connect with other learners with similar passions, and share their passion work with the world. We want students to know that whether their interest is baseball or baking cakes, there are people all over the world who will share that interest.

The minimum requirements for the Class Blog are as follows, with options for students to add their own creativity.

Assignment Example: Introduce yourself and your passion, interest, or hobby, etc.

♦ Provide photos or create a digital story of your project.

♦ Create a video describing their passion or project.

♦ Create a comic strip.

Provide something original: Get creative and add a component or content which differs from the tasks listed above. It might be an extra page presenting some interesting content you made or wrote yourself, or which provides links to sites you have found useful while making the site, or which are about related or relevant subjects. or it might be something made with a tool you have researched and learned to use yourself.

If enjoying the topic and sharing your expertise aren't enough to show you the benefits of blogging about your passion, what else is there to gain? That's simple:

♦ You have value and expertise you can offer to others.

♦ You can share personal experiences that will help people relate to your content and connect with your words.

♦ You will be excited to share new thoughts and discoveries with your readers.

What you'll also start to notice is that you become an authority in your niche, and this is highly valuable. With this authority you can release products, offer coaching or set-up a popular paid membership site depending on your industry. This is so much harder to do in saturated markets where there is a lot of competition. The beauty of the Internet is that it allows people with similar interests (no matter how obscure) to find each other faster and easier, without barriers of time or geography.

The Passion Portfolio

Artists, architects, designers, and photographers, for example, keep portfolios of their best work. Students can benefit from keeping a portfolio of your work. The portfolio is important as evidence of accomplishment, and it is also important as an instrument of self-motivation. Knowing you are going to present your work in your portfolio as evidence of what you have done and can do, you are likely to choose challenging work and finish it as skillfully as you can.

We suggest that the following items be in the Portfolio:

- Project Planning Template

- Project Resources

- Samples of the work—writing, photographs, storyboards, notes from the Learning Journal

Passion Project Planning:

On page 122, you will find a Planning Sheet to help your students get started on their Passion Projects.

Passion Project: Planning Sheet

Name: _____ Date: _____

Think about something that you have a passion for and would like to explore:

What do you know a lot about?

_____

_____

What do you wonder about?

_____

_____

What do you love to do?

_____

_____

Our project can be ANY topic of your choice. Talk to your friends and family this week and ask them:

Getting Started:

What do you already know a lot about?

_____

What do you want most to learn more about?

_____

What question do you have?

_____

Project Research Log:

I have gotten more information about my topic by:

Reading these books:

_____

Exploring these websites:

_____

Interviewing this expert:

_____

Visiting these places:

_____

Other:

_____

7

From the Trenches: The Voices of Passion

I imagine a school system that recognizes learning is natural, that a love of learning is normal, and that real learning is passionate learning.

—Tom Peters Author 'Re-imagine'

Educators are a conscientious, caring group of professionals. With very few exceptions, their dedication and efforts are exemplary. As teaching and learning are steadily directed away from passion by well-meaning policy makers, however, teachers are confused and frustrated. Educators today are deeply divided about the heart of our system. We live in a time of major conflict in which many embrace an emerging way of seeing the world while others among us defend the traditions of how school used to be. The authors have struggled personally and professionally with what to call these two philosophies of learning and being. We conclude that the difference is foundational.

A Webinar with Sir Ken Robinson

As the first decade of the 21st century neared its end, thousands of global educators had the chance to voice their thoughts, feelings, and opinions about passion and its place in their work. World acclaimed education author and passion expert, Sir Ken Robinson, joined us in a live and interactive webinar to discuss his latest book, *The Element: How Finding Your Passion Changes Everything,* and offered provocative thought such as these:

♦ Does passion = good teaching? Can you be a "good teacher" without it?

♦ Passion isn't something that is created but rather the results of the conditions under which learning is allowed to occur.

- To awaken "passion," we must broaden our focus to incorporate time to play, tinker, experiment, EXPLORE.

- Sometimes I think that my passion for what I do is what makes my job HARDER!

- It takes one that is passionate about learning in order to be passionate about teaching.

- Burnout is possible for passionate teachers—especially if they often feel unappreciated; luckily, recharging can happen.

- So do you have passion? When you go into your classroom or your school or your district, do your colleagues know you have passion? More important, do your students know it?

Educators attending the webinar questioned how to define, quantify, and maintain passion in light of today's educational challenges. Some educators noted that teaching to the test and its subsequent restrictions has diminished the freedom of educators to teach creatively and their own passion to teach as well. Some disagree, stating that this lack of freedom actually ignites passion in educators.

The discussion was, well, passionate. Here is a taste of what went on. The following transcript represents the real-time conversation that occurred on Twitter before the live session began:

The conversation began with this tweet: What do you think about passion in education? Leave a comment!

@rliberni – The topic today is passion in education and how that can drive change.

Many of us are the change agents at our school site or district level and it's ironic that when they call us experts and so knowledgeable I immediately smile inside and think, "if only you had your own PLN or participated in some virtual community or discussion such as #edchat, because there are some brilliant minds out there sharing, challenging, and altering my learning on a daily basis."

✳ Two important questions that were asked early in the chat were:

@rliberni – Does passion always come from the teacher? and How can we define passion?

✳ And the responses were just as interesting:

@MatthiasHeil – To me, passion is what makes us tick, and explore—even at great cost. Has to do with teaching, I guess...)

@joe_bower – Passion is a love for something for its own sake and someone couldn't stop you from doing it if they tried

@AngelaMaiers – Passion the force that exists allowing one 2 commit fully 2 the job, task, or cause—across any challenge or obstacle

@MatthiasHeil – Passion can neither be created nor taught, it can only be encouraged...

@teachingwthsoul – Passion is the unrelenting pursuit of what you strongly believe in

And perhaps an idea that touches upon a person becoming a teacher as a calling, a spiritual pursuit

@stevejmoore – Passion = suffering = delay of pleasure. So passionate people do delay their own pleasure for thing else.

@AngelaMaiers – Passion without drive, without suffering, is called a hobby

@kylepace – absolutely—passion-driven learning has a whole lot more to do with drive than it does fun and engagement

@jasonfloam – passion is an overwhelming driving desire to make a difference. It requires challenging y'self & then others 2 engage

@jenwagner@AngelaMaiers – passion is a personal emotion/attitude/belief that can have a positive effect on so many others (or bug them as well) :)

@pammoran – those things can situationally support emergence of passion, be outcomes of passion—but could it be passion is fire?

✴ The conversation also took a look at ways teachers can create passion.

@MissCheska – I believe passion comes from both the teacher and students—learning is shared & valued together
@rliberni – I agree both 'feed' off each other this is crucial to learning I think

@cybraryman1 – Attending/Presenting at conferences & workshops. Meeting like-minded fellow educators increases your passion.
@rliberni – true passion can be nurtured by students, colleagues and PLNs

* Teachers did a great job of making the case for why passion is important in 140 characters.

@PGRoom209 – I think the amount of passion is the difference between teachers who continually improve and those who don't.

@MissCheska – Passion = persistence

and perhaps more importantly

@kevcreutz – Even when you fail. RT @

MissCheska – #edchat Passion = persistence

* This idea of allowing failure and treating it as something to let our students grow by needs to be looked at more closely. Many seemed to agree that passion helps educators overcome systemic focuses that are not related to learning.

* The chat also began to move to more of a cautious examination of passion with perhaps so much unbridled enthusiasm when:

@tomwhitby – Can Passion distract us from Reason? Just because we are passionate about something does it make it right?

@web20classroom – I think we have to be careful. Too often in history we see passion that is misguided…

but followed up with

@web20classroom – All the educators must teach with passion

It felt like the discussion of some primal force that propels us and drives us to be teachers and needs to also be reflected upon even as our actions seem the right thing to do.

* And for me the question in regards to educators around me that don't share in my drive and enthusiasm:

@michellek107 – Good question – is it automatic or learned? RT

@tomwhitby – How do we promote Passion?

Derrall Garrison, fifth-grade elementary teacher in the Cupertino Union School District, summarizes the experience with his honest and heartfelt response here:

I always preface a conversation with someone when they enter my classroom with "it's my passion" when trying to explain why I have so many computers and want to talk incessantly about project-based learning, using blogs and wikis to build community in the classroom and other essential 21st-century skills that can seem arcane to the average visitor.

It sometimes can feel like a path that I alone walk. How else to explain the feeling when I've been at four school sites within ten years and have only once been able to convince, cajole, or find someone that wants their students to even blog. Someone once told me that if I were to go too far back in working in a classroom with my staff's perspective in mind I would lose motivation and they were probably right.

Even now that I lead professional development sessions in my district and school site and raise the pitch of my voice or try and project all the energy I can muster, it's disheartening to see the look of disinterest and loss of attention. I'd give anything for a group of teachers coming up all excited as learners passionate and starry-eyed with the possibilities. But this is why I enjoy teaching children, they still have that spark of curiosity, the ability to become passionate and the willingness for change that I find lacking in many teachers.

As with any powerful conversation, we left with more questions than we came with, questions like:

♦ One fear I have is that as my learning is altered and accelerates and pushes me to reflect and informs my passion, how will I communicate with my colleagues who choose not to change?

♦ Will many of us always be part of a group of educators who will have to look outside our schools and districts for change and passion?

✱ The learning did not stop with our questions, as the community generously shared resources, links, and suggestions, continuing to seek answers:

@cybraryman1 – Teaching is not a profession; it's a passion. Ed. Quotes – http://bit.ly/EPRmh

@joe_bower – I wrote this last night in anticipation of today's passion/Sir Ken Robinson talk on #edchat http://bit.ly/9MREpU I am passionate about this!

@Edu4U – Good read on the changing face of the University http://budurl.com/q2kq

@R4RLA – Collaborate with professionals to renew your passion! Attend/ present at our conferences http://bit.ly/ccP37Q

@malcolmbellamy – for a short introduction to Sir Ken Robinson's ideas see http://bit.ly/aXl6AQ

@MikeGwaltney – Most people are more afraid of Failure than Mediocrity. It should be the reverse. http://bit.ly/9dhrUh @danielpink

@akenuam – what teachers make – http://bit.ly/27oCDA

@web20education – Teachers connect with other teacher

@ShellTerrel – passion #edchat http://web20ineducation2010.ning.com/ video/web-20-and-new-tehnologies-in

@tomwhitby – Upon the conclusion of #edchat watch this video on leadership. It fosters passion in followers. http://bit.ly/b9b6M4

@isteconnects – ETAN needs teacher advocates to tell Congress their stories. Share your passion! http://bit.ly/9enJ8M

@graingered – We (teachers) look far & wide 4 solutions in education… we R the SOLUTION! We need to find our passion! http://tinyurl.com/ ydhkd8r

@DUMACORNELLUCIA – Here is a cool TEDtalk on passion in education. Very cool story from India http://bit.ly/9cFfR1

I posted the following comment on my blog just minutes after the conversation ended:

> I fall asleep tonight with a smile on my face knowing that **passion is alive and well in the world of teaching and learning**. Nearly 500 more joined us for the main event, breaking an all- time record for Elluminate and Learn Central, and confirming what I suspect you already know to be true: Passion Matters! Lots to dream about here!

Margaret Meed said it best: Do not underestimate the power of a small group of passionate individuals in their ability to change the world. If you have not had a chance to participate in a conversation like this, you can begin any time. Here are a few quick tips:

New to Edchat?

If you have never participated in an #Edchat discussion, these take place twice a day every Tuesday on Twitter. Over 800 educators participate in this discussion by just adding #edchat to their tweets. For tips on participating in the discussion, please check out these posts!

♦ **Edchat: Join the Conversation** at http://teacherbootcamp.edublogs.org/2009/08/18/edchat-join-the-conversation/

♦ **Using Tweetdeck for Hashtag Discussions** at http://teacherboot-camp.edublogs.org/2009/09/01/edchat-update-using-tweetdeck-for-hashtag-discussions/

More Edchat

♦ If you would like to join others in transforming the discussion into action, please feel free to join the Edchat group on the Educator PLN ning at http://edupln.ning.com/group/edchat

♦ Jerry Swiatek (http://twitter.com/jswiatek) does an incredible job of posting each archived transcript (http://edchat.pbworks.com/Side-Bar) on the Edchat wiki created by Steve Johnson (http://twitter.com/edtechsteve). This way you can look back at your favorites!

♦ Follow other Edchatters and make sure you are on this Twitter list if you participate in Edchat! (See http://twitter.com/ShellTerrell/edchat.)

♦ Read summaries of the 7pm EST/1 am CET Edchat discussions at http://web20classroom.blogspot.com/search/label/edchat.

Challenge

If you're new to hashtag discussions, then just show up on Twitter on any Tuesday and add just a few tweets on the topic with the hashtag #edchat.

You can see the entire passion discussion at http://edchat.pbworks.com/3302010+-+7PM+EDT+-+Passion+in+Education-Lead-in+to+Sir+Ken+Robinson+webcast. We encourage you to read it and to also check out the archive (http://www.learncentral.org/node/60493) of the Sir Ken Robinson webinar. Well worth an hour of your time. We want to thank @betty-ray from Edutopia for capturing and sharing this amazing conversation with the community (http://www.edutopia.org/spiralnotebook/betty-ray).

8

Closing Thoughts: Choosing Passion in Times of Change

We started this book with a specific agenda; to make the case: Passion Matters. Passion is more than an icing on the cake; a luxury we engage in when time permits. Passion *is* the cake.

This book represents what we believe about passion. It represents what teachers have told us and what we witness to be true in the world. Even so, we believe our case for passion is best made by those we seek to teach.

Children are the most passionate, ravenous, fearless learners we know. They are insatiably curious, innately fearless, and they WANT to learn! If our schools are to be places where passionate and powerful learning happens, children should have a thing or two to say about what they need.

We have had the great pleasure and honor of bringing passion into the conversation with hundreds of students. This represents the message they have sent us about what matters most, what they will remember, and what they need from us. With their permission, we share it with you. Accordingly, its title is "The Promise of Passion."

Read this twice, once for the mind and once for the heart.

The Promise of Passion

Dear Teacher,

Love me.
Make me feel special.
Make me feel included.
Make me feel valued.

Smile for me.
Tell me that you're happy to see me.
Tell me that you're happy to teach me.
Tell me that you're happy I am here.

Involve me.
Tell me about our work together.
Tell me how I can be of help and mean it genuinely.

Notice me.
See all of me.
See my emotions, my laughter, my curiosity, my anticipation.
See my right, and I will work on the "wrongs."

Teach me.
PLEASE don't just tell me what you know.
Show me what I need to know.
Show me how to do it well.

Help Me.
Help me when it gets hard.
Help me persevere.
Help me know it matters.

Excite Me.
I came to you in love with learning.
Keep me excited!
Show me the fun.
Show me your fire and passion.

Promise Me.
Promise me that you can.
Promise me that you will
Promise me that you are ready to...
Love me, help me, engage me, excite me, and teach me.

I'm ready for you.
I want to learn.
I want to know.
I want to be your student.

I PROMISE, I will return the favor
I will reward you with my attention, my focus, my heart
I will show you what I can do
I will show you who I can be.

PROMISE ME?

What did you hear? What can we learn from their voices? How did students address:

Standards?

Learning Theory?

Rigor?

Relevant, real life application?

Curriculum and Instruction?

Challenge and Perseverance?

What did you hear about teaching and learning theory?

Motivation?

Engagement?

PASSION?

We are lucky. We get to spend time at our work doing what we are passionate about. Not many people get to say that. With all the opportunity and possibility the 21st century offers us, very few people are living in what Sir Ken Robinson refers to as their "element": the place where our passions and talents meet.

Given what we know about students, the system, and the world, can we afford to promise them any less?

Closing Thoughts:
Choosing Passion in Times of Change

He who chooses the beginning of a road chooses the place it leads to. It is the means that determine the end.

—Harry Emerson Rosdick

In some ways the process of putting this book together symbolizes the end of a path, but the journey does not end here. We knew in advance that there is no end of the road, no higher power with a magic wand to solve our problems, but we also knew what we can do using passion as a source for both energy and inspiration.

We admit there are days when mustering up passion is no easy task. There are even days where leaving the classroom and the field seems like the best path to take. But when we lie in bed at night thinking about the future, we know we are on the right path; doing the right thing for our students and ourselves. And we know we NEED passion to continue the course:

- ◆ We need teachers who care about kids.

- ◆ We need educators who have passion for learning themselves and want to foster that love in their students.

- ◆ We need teachers who have a fire in their belly for learning and discovery and teachers who want their kids to experience the same.

Passion is a choice. And choosing passion in a time of insurmountable change will not be easy. Change is hard. It is human instinct to resist it as we find comfort in things steady and predictable. However, steady and predictable are not words that describe the world our students live in. Attempts to shift the current paradigm and inject passion-driven practices is not for the faint at heart.

Choosing passion is an act of defiance as it asks us to defy perfection, predictability, and safe, scripted teaching. Committing to passion means being vulnerable and wrong. It will require you to exercise strength and embrace the struggle as you nurture connections and welcome new challenges.

Today, we invite you to choose passion. We invite you to live and teach with your whole heart and soul. We need your momentum and energy in this passion-driven movement. We need to be surrounded by activists and advocates who are willing to be imperfect and real. We need to build a community of passionate people who are both afraid and brave. Today we invite you to take the first step.

References

Atwell, N. (2007). *The reading zone: How to help kids become skilled, passionate, habitual, critical readers*. New York: Scholastic.

Boushy, G., & Moser, J. (2006). *The daily five: Fostering literacy independence in the elementary grades*. Portland, ME: Stenhouse.

Dewey, J. (1944). *Democracy and education*. New York: Simon & Schuster.

Feldhusen, J. F., & Treffinger, D. J. (1975). Teachers' attitudes and practices in teaching creativity and problem solving to economically disadvantaged and minority children. *Psychological Reports, 37*, 1161–1162.

Fountas, I., & Pinnell, G. (1999). *Matching books to readers*. Portsmouth, NH: Heinemann.

Fried, R. (2005). *The game of school: Why we all play it, how it hurts kids, and what it will take to change it*. San Francisco: Jossey-Bass.

Friedman, T. (2008). *The world is flat: A brief history of the twenty-first century*. New York: Farrar, Straus and Giroux

Graves, D. (2003). *Writing: Teachers & children at work*. Portsmouth, NH: Heinemann.

Graves, D. (1990). *Discover your own literacy*. Portsmouth, NH: Heinemann.

Hargreaves, A. (1994). *Changing teachers, changing times: Teachers work and culture in the postmodern age*. London: Cassell.

Harvey, S., & Goudvis, A. (2007). *Strategies that work (2nd ed.)*. Portland, ME: Stenhouse.

Heard, G. (1999). *Awakening the heart: Exploring poetry in elementary and middle school*. Portsmouth, NH: Heinemann.

AU: Not found in text.

Kaufman, D. (2002, July). Living a literate life, revisited. *JSTOR: The English Journal, 91*(6), 51–57.

Keene, E., & Zimmermann (1997). *Mosaic of thought: Teaching comprehension in a reader's workshop*. Portsmouth, NH: Heinemann.

Meyer, R. (2006). *Frontloading the core curriculum*. Available at http://www.donjohnston.com/pdf/incite/Incite_White_Paper.pdf (Incite! Learning Series).

Neumann, A. (2009). Protecting the passion of scholars in times of change. *Change: The Magazine of Higher Learning*. Interview with Professor Richard

Marin. Can also be found on the web at http://www.changemag.org/Archives/Back%20Issues/March-April%202009/full-protecting-the-passion.html

Osterman, K. (2000). Students' need for belongingness in the school community. *Review of Educational Research, 70*(3), 323–367.

Palmer, P. (1998). *The courage to teach: Exploring the inner landscape of a teacher's life*. San Franciso: Jossey-Bass.

The Partnership for 21st Century Skills. (2008). Tuscon, AZ. Available at http://www.21stcenturyskills.org.

Reeves, D. (2010). *Transforming professional development into student results*. Alexandria, VA: Association for Supervision and Curriculum Development.

Robinson, K. & Aronica, L. *The Element: How Finding Your Passion Changes Everything*. New York: Penguin

Routman, R. (2002). *Reading Essentials*. Portsmouth, NH: Heinemann.

Routman, R. (1996). *Literacy at the crossroads: Crucial talk about reading, writing, and other teaching dilemmas*. Portsmouth, NH: Heinemann.

Serafini, F. (2004). *Lessons in comprehension: Explicit instruction in the reading workshop*. NH: Heinemann. Available at http://issuu.com/publishgold/docs/chapter163.

Sollman, C., Emmons, B., & Paolini, J. (1994). *Through the cracks*. New York: Sterling.

Stoksky, S. "A Challenge to the Partnership for 21st Century Skills." Available at http://www.commoncore.org/p21-challenge.php.

Wagner, T. (2008). *The Global Achievement Gap.* New York: Basic Books.

Westby, E., & Dawson, V. L. (1995). Creativity: Asset or burden in the classroom? *Creative Research Journal, 18*(1), 10.

Willingham, Dan. (2009, March 26). "How Can We Get Students to Think Like Experts," Available at http://www.coreknowledge.com.

Notes

Notes